PSYCHOANALYTIC IDEAS
AND SHAKESPEARE

Psychoanalytic Ideas and Shakespeare is one of a series of low-cost books under the title PSYCHOANALYTIC **ideas** which brings together the best of Public Lectures and other writings given by analysts of the British Psycho-Analytical Society on important psychoanalytic subjects.

The books can be ordered from:
Karnac Books
www.karnacbooks.com
Tel. +(0)20 8969 4454
Fax: +(0)20 8969 5585
E-mail: shop@karnacbooks.com

Other titles in the Psychoanalytic Ideas Series:

Shame and Jealousy: The Hidden Turmoils
Phil Mollon

Dreaming and Thinking
Rosine Jozef Perelberg (editor)

Spilt Milk: Perinatal Loss and Breakdown
Joan Raphael-Leff (editor)

Unconscious Phantasy
Riccardo Steiner (editor)

Psychosis (Madness)
Paul Williams (editor)

Adolescence
Inge Wise (editor)

Child Analysis Today
Luis Rodríguez de la Sierra (editor)

PSYCHOANALYTIC IDEAS AND SHAKESPEARE

Editors

Inge Wise and Maggie Mills

Series Editors

Inge Wise and *Paul Williams*

KARNAC

LONDON   NEW YORK

First published in 2006 by
H. Karnac (Books) Ltd.
6 Pembroke Buildings, London NW10 6RE

British Library Cataloguing in Publication Data

A C.I.P. for this book is available from the British Library

  ISBN 1 85575 334 0

Edited, typeset and produced by The Studio Publishing Services Ltd, www.publishingservicesuk.co.uk
e-mail: studio@publishingservicesuk.co.uk

Printed in Great Britain by Hobbs the Printers Ltd, Totton, Hampshire

10 9 8 7 6 5 4 3 2 1

www.karnacbooks.com

CONTENTS

Peter Hildebrand—in memoriam

ACKNOWLEDGEMENTS

We wish to thank all those whose ideas and efforts have contributed to this volume for their support. Most of all the authors for their patience, the reviewers for their thoughtful suggestions, Hannah Gardener and Nick Hall at the Institute of Psycho-Analysis, and Max and Theo Hildebrand. Inge Wise also wishes to express her appreciation to Adam Wise, her medium in most things web-based, for his tireless addiction to Arden.

Peter Buckroyd has a Doctorate in English Literature and is a free-lance Educational Consultant who has published widely in literature and education. His main field is Assessment.

Michael Conran worked as a psychiatrist in the NHS. Psychosis and borderline were areas of special interest to him, as was analysis, understanding and treatment of schizophrenia, the subject of his MD. He was equally interested in literature. He was a member of the British Psychoanalytical Society. He chaired the Applied Section and Public Lectures. The Psychoanalytic Ideas series grew out of his suggestion to publish in book form three public lectures on adolescence. He died in 2002.

Peter Hildebrand, Independent Training Analyst of the British Psychoanalytical Society and Member of Council. He worked for many years as Chief Consultant Psychologist in the Adult Department of the Tavistock Clinic as well as in private practice. He has held professorships at the University of Brunel and North-western, Chicago. His best known book is *Beyond the Mid-Life Crisis*. He published many clinical papers as well as work on brief

psychotherapy, life-span psychology, AIDS and HIV patients, analytic training and supervision, Lacan, Derrida and contemporary
French psychoanalysis, and papers on the relations between psychoanalysis and theatre and literature. He died in 2001.

Maggie Mills studied Jurisprudence at Oxford, trained at the Royal
Free Hospital in London, and then worked as a Consultant Clinical
Psychologist in the NHS. She is now retired and works in private
practice. She qualified as a psychoanalyst and is a Professor of
Developmental Psychology at the University of Syracuse. She
helped to found a psychotherapy service in Brixton for women
from ethnic minorities, and also worked for many years with
Newpin. She publishes on maternal depression, domestic violence,
parent—child relationships and psychotherapeutic change. Her cur-
rent interest, as a Director of Mellow Parenting, is in helping fami-
lies in difficult circumstances to parent their young children.

Inge Wise trained in marital and adult psychotherapy at the
Tavistock Clinic prior to becoming a psychoanalyst and a member
of the British Psycho-Analytic Society. She works in private practice, lectures, teaches, and supervises in this country and abroad.
She studied English, French, and Spanish Literature, and worked as
a simultaneous interpreter. She is fluent in several languages. She
started the Psychoanalytic Ideas series, which she edits with
Professor Paul Williams. *Adolescence*, edited by her and published
in this series, has been reprinted in 2004.

Gerald Wooster trained at the Maudsley Hospital and qualified at
the British Psychoanalyical Society. He was Consultant Psychotherapist at St.George's Hospital Medical School. He has contributed to *Student Health, Forensic Psychotherapy, Matte Blanco's
BiLogic, Sibling Dynamics,* and drawn attention to the importance of
Shakespeare for psychotherapists. He has retired from the NHS and
works in private practice. He plans, with Peter Buckroyd, to publish a book on the influence of real loss in Shakespeare's life and
work.

Introduction

Maggie Mills

When I was a child my father ran a printing works a few miles down river from Shakespeare's home town. For years he published all the Stratford Theatre programmes. It was also the place where I spent Fridays while my mother got on with running the household.

I used to be mesmerized watching kirtled and wimpoled heroines in gorgeous brocades bow to doublet and hosed gentlemen in gaudy velvets as they twirled above my head, immortalized on the programme pages whizzing by on overhead conveyor belts. When things got hectic, I was shooed off to the cool and musky bookbinding room where I opened up each glossy programme, always to find an account of a Shakespeare play. Articles on learned textual criticism surely escaped me, but I must have had most of Shakespeare's dramatic personae by heart. My pet rabbit was known as Feste, the Christmas goose one year was designated Pericles, I had an imaginary friend called Orlando, who lived in the game larder, and I remember the comptroller of the local gymkhana looked a bit startled when I said my pony's name was Goneril.

Each time I looked into a programme, I encountered an exotic, imaginary world. Illyria was my favourite, such a lovely word, I thought, and as Peter Hildebrand points out in his text, close to our word, "illusion". These were entirely new landscapes, full of surprises, but I can see now they blended in with my country childhood. I could try to follow the narrative as Shakespeare had intended, or make up my own stories as I went along. As a rather solitary child, it all felt very real to me and hardly make-believe at all. After all, what is fact and what fiction? They always elide in our internal world.

I think it was also from Stratford's Bard that I learnt that the important stories are always about passion: the intimate violence of family life and the unbearable poignancy of lost, loved ones. Shakespeare never forgets the drama of that thin tight-rope that governs all our lives between safety and danger. "There is a widespread feeling that psychoanalytic thought has a particular kinship with the work of Shakespeare" (Sokol, 1993, p. 3). A perceived kinship, not just because Freud himself was inspired by reading Shakespeare but, as Sokol puts it, "because in Shakespeare's work, as in psychoanalytic work, there is a profound sense of how the unconscious processes that develop our capacities for love and concern underlie all other aspects of human life" (ibid.).

Patients always seem amazed that analysts can remember so much about them. Not just the essence of how if feels to be with them, but so many details of their personal archives. On first meeting a patient it feels, at least to me, as if they are presenting their own play or opening up a new novel to be shared. I hope it does not sound disrespectful to say we are privileged to witness literature "on the hoof". Human minds are uniquely fashioned, I think, to find people's stories compelling. I'm sure most analysts on their deathbed could still give a good account of the dramatic personae and dynamics of every patient they treated.

As Sodre (2000, p.1) points out "psychoanalysts concern themselves at every moment in their work with listening to, thinking about, and commenting on a particular form of narrative that is simultaneously factual and fictional; the analysts task of sympathetic understanding involves examining the relationship between phantasy and reality". These personal archives when opened up are about a particular kind of memory, namely the psychological distortions of true experience. A myriad of different readings are explored, again and again throughout an analysis as concsious and unconscious conflicts are discovered and worked with until, with luck, the unconscious boulders patients have themselves strewn in their path to avoid painful truths get pushed aside or no longer need to be stumbled over. Sodre talks of "powerful unconscious 'plots' which inform the way we feel" (*ibid.*, p.14) and when worked with and understood a better object relations for the patient may result.

MacDougall (1986) likewise talks of a number of characters in our own little universe that are

> parts of ourselves that frequently operate in complete contradiction to one another, causing conflict and mental pain to our conscious selves. for we are relatively unacquainted with these hidden players and their roles. Whether we will it or not, our inner characters are constantly seeking a stage on which to play out their tragedies and comedies. Although we rarely assume responsibility for our secret theatre productions, the producer is seated in our own minds. Moreover, it is this inner world with its repeating repertory that determines most of what happens to us in the external world. [p. 2]

Freud seized on the notion that there is "another theatre in the mind—'der andere Schauplatz'", which differs from ordinary waking life and governs the production of dreams and other unconscious ideation. Hildebrand, in this volume makes the link between the theatre in everyday life and the internal theatre in each of us— "the stage on which we enact and re-enact our psychological dramas."

It is his thesis that "there exist an infinite number of reflections between the inner theatre of phantasy and the external theatre of everyday life and that examination of plays in these terms will permit us, without interfering with the actual effect of the piece, to increase and deepen our response to the play." A good example of what he means is provided by Michael Ignatieff in a National Theatre programme. He offers an account of his differing transference to King Lear at various stages of his life, prompted by Ian Holm's recent interpretation of the role. "What we think Lear is about depends on how old we are, how much we have lived." As a sixteen-year-old schoolboy he saw it as being all about cruelty. In his twenties, it got more complicated. Seeing the play then, he said, triggered "a revealingly guilty reflex". He sympathized with Lear

although his own behaviour to his parents at the time was pre-
dominantly "standard ingratitude". Years later, and now a parent
himself, he could accept that Lear was really an "impossible old
man", and one completely "unreconciled" to being old. Confused
and bloodyminded, he will go to his grave that way—just as Robert
Stephens played the role at Stratford quite shortly before his own
death.

Ignatieff's (1997) illustration is rich with contrary identifications
and he gives a sense of the reality of Shakespeare's fictional cre-
ations for him, which resemble radically real things that correspond
to his own internal landscape. Shakespeare's play gave meaning to
his own emotional experiences and I deliberately mention the
actors who actually fostered this process because they are the protagonists so often passed over in commentaries of this kind. Hildebrand, in this volume, comments further on the intricacies of
theatrical performance and its close resemblance to the process of
an analytic sesssion, when he says "Both psychoanalysis and the
theatre provide a determinedly neutral but also clearly circumscribed repetitive situation and favour the expression of internal
feelings and relationships, which cannot at the beginning be plainly
defined but are clearly understood as the products of an interaction
between the participants. Furthermore, both psychoanalysis and
theatre are staged in a formal and clearly defined way, either in the
theatrical space or in the consulting room, and each is insistently
repetitive in nature. Neither can be guaranteed to work on every
occasion and the audience and the performances can never interact
in exactly the same way. Nevertheless, there is something in the
repetition and the framework that enables us to get to grips with
the internal world in a revolutionary way". Hildebrand's proviso,
and it is an important one, is that psychoanalysis and plays,
whether read or viewed, can benefit each provided they do not try
to go beyond the single case method.

Finally, before giving a brief account of each chapter, it is appropriate, since most papers in this volume represent the Independent
Group in contemporary British Psychoanalysis, to remind readers of
Donald Winnicott's thinking on the relation between analysis and
literary works of arts: the potential space of play (and, by analogy,
the plays of Shakespeare). He contends (1971, p. 118) that: "Play is in
fact neither a matter of inner psychic reality nor a matter of external

reality. The place where cultural experience is located is in the *potential* space between the individual and the environment". When we enter such a potential space in thinking about and working with our patients, when this in its turn can be related in the mind of both the analyst and/or the patient to such lived cultural experience as a play or a film, then the combination of these two hermeneutics offer us the potentiality of mutual enrichment.

In "Psychoanalysis and theatre", Hildebrand uses *Twelfth Night* as a vehicle to convey the many facets generated in the space between the phantasy of the inner and the reality of the outer worlds. Prevalent in the play are themes of primal phantasies concerning love and gender identity, including expressions by Shakespeare of his own internal landscape (fathering twins, one of whom died at childbirth, and addressing the lack of paternal investment in his life, his own father dying when the author was still young). By overlaying the Freudian theory of love on to this classic depiction of romantic love, we can understand better both our responses to the play itself, which are in turns both painful and frightening, humorous and temporary, and the interaction of the "many-mirrored" inner space with the flat and less enthralling outer space of personality.

In "Grief, loss, and creativity: whither the Phoenix?" Wooster and Buckroyd contend that creativity can follow from loss: they "distinguish between the destructive and more creative sequelae of loss".

Frequent responses to grievous loss are manic defence and depression. Wooster and Buckroyd examine psychoanalytic concepts that "provide a framework for thinking about creativity".

Grief, anger, guilt, envy, jealousy, and shame all play their part in the mourning process, and it is our ability to face our responses to these that will determine its outcome.

The authors discuss Rothenberg's *The Emerging Goddess* as "one of the most comprehensive descriptions of the common factors of creativity". This is followed by their consideration "of the group as a crucible in which grief, loss. and creativity can be expressed in different ways".

Last, they bring Shakespeare's *All's Well That Ends Well* as the play that "binds together grief, loss, and creativity in its own content and in the circumstances surrounding its composition and context".

In "The Caledonian tragedy", Hildebrand peers into the murky depths of Shakespeare's most theatrically superstitious play to uncover the taboo of mother–son incest symbolically represented between Macbeth and Lady Macbeth, whose moral ambivalence in their quest for power and the fulfilment of ambition leads them to bloody murder and eventual disaster. An unnatural malice inherent in the play—the moral ambivalence, the reversal of values, the disrupting of natural order and the barren consequences of murder and betrayal—is added to by Hildebrand's psychoanalytical reading of the symbolic representation of an incestuous relationship between Macbeth and Lady Macbeth, which he argues is consummated by the patricide of Duncan, the symbolic father figure.

Peter Hall (1982) argues "The dramatisation of the relationship between Lady Macbeth and Macbeth *makes* the story happen", and by uncovering such a culturally proscribed act at its centre, Hildebrand presents us with a hidden meaning which provides understanding to the play's perpetual unluckiness and horrific power.

In "Considerations of shame, guilt and forgiveness", Michael Conran draws attention to the fact that the state of the relationship we have to our inner objects will determine how we will be able to think about our own death and dying.

This relies foremost on our "capacity for self-forgiveness". Conran argues that when this capacity exists then "the admission of guilt is possible, as distinct from shame, which is seen to excite the defences of denial, splitting, and projection."

Taking the "madness and death of King Lear" as his example, he shows "how skilfully Shakespespeare directs our attention to the difficulties man encounters in taking responsibility for his mental life, if he is to anticipate a peaceful and dignified exit".

In "The other side of the wall", Hildebrand addresses the phenomenon of creativity in later life drawing on several Shakespeare plays and Auden's poetic response to his last play, *The Tempest*, entitled *The Sea and the Mirror*. He presents a theory of creativity based on object-relations and structuralist accounts of myth. Foreshadowing by fifteen years his "Prospero's book", which is also included in this volume, he emphasizes the importance of the playwright's acceptance of his own mortality and his renunciation of illusion as a defence against the fear of death. He deals with some of the dramatist's own personal psychological themes that Shakespeare worked and reworked throughout his life; for example oedipal issues in *Hamlet* and generativity and renunciation in *The Tempest*. Hildebrand concludes with the statement that "creativity is not just about life, it is about death as well".

In "Prospero's book", Hildebrand proposes that the interplay between the hermeneutics of psychoanalysis and theatre can illuminate understanding of the transference and countertransference in a long psychoanalysis with a young woman whose disturbance was so severe from early sexual abuse in childhood and adolescent anorexia that her life was endangered by repeated suicide attempts. In understanding the oedipal bond between analyst and patient, Hildebrand draws on a rich reading of Shakespeare's *Tempest*, involving the object relations of Prospero and Miranda. The interweaving of fantasy, poetry, and magic in the play fires Hildebrand's own imagination in helping him to relinquish his own omnipotence and immortality in the face of his own imminent death towards the end of the analysis. As he says "It is very hard for an analyst to give up his powers", let alone be prepared to discuss the subject publicly in a truly analytic way. As Miranda is released into independence and a satisfying sexual life in the play, and his patient comes to replace destructive inner objects with more reparative and benign ones as she develops a capacity for concern and mourning of her analyst's approaching death, so Hildebrand very movingly describes surrendering his analytic role—"breaking his staff . . . and drowning his book".

References

Auden, W. H. (1944). *The Sea and the Mirror, A Commentary on Shakespeare's* The Tempest. A. Kirsch (Ed.). Princeton, NJ: Oxford University Press, reprinted 2003.

Hall, P. (1982). Interview with John Russell Brown. In: J. R. Brown (Ed.), *Focus on Macbeth* (pp. 8–35). London: Routledge & Kegan Paul.

Ignatieff, M. (1997). *From Blindness to Sight*. London: Nick Hern.

MacDougall, J. (1986). *Theatres of the Mind: Illusion and Truth on the Analytic Stage*. London: Free Association.

Sodre, I. (2000). Psychoanalysis and literature. Paper presented to the British Psychoanalytical Society, London.

Sokol, B. J. (1993).*The Undiscovered Country: New Essays on Psychoanalysis and Shakespeare*. London Free Association.

Winnicott, D. W. (1971). *Playing and Reality*. London: Faber.

CHAPTER ONE

Psychoanalysis and theatre

Peter Hildebrand

T he title of this chapter is "Psychoanalysis and theatre".
Serious academic scholars and theatre professionals will
know more about theatre than I do. However, I was a paid-
up member of the American Federation of Radio Actors in my
youth, one of my sons is a professional actor, and I have analysed
several eminent actors. If you follow *MASH*, you will remember
that the psychiatrist to the hospital is Dr Hildebrand. This was no
accident—so that I do have at least a nodding acquaintance with
the theatre and with acting. From the analytic point of view, I have
been a training analyst for over twenty-five years and a member of
the Independent Group of the British Psychoanalytical Society.
Please note that while I have established some credentials in relation to my title, I have not yet mentioned the second word in the
title—that little conjunction "and". In some ways, it is the most
important word of the three and may lead us in some interesting
directions.

Ernest Jones, in his biography of Freud (1980), tells us that he
was "ill-informed in the field of contemporary psychology", and
seems to have derived mainly from hearsay any knowledge that he
may have had of it. Freud often admitted this ignorance, although

later work has shown that he was familiar with the notion first put forward by the mid-Victorian philosopher, Herbart, that "ideas are primary to affects". Jones gives a very interesting account of Herbart's ideas—saying that he conceived of two thresholds in the mind which correspond with Freud's ideas. One is the static threshold, where an inhibited idea is robbed of its activity and can enter consciousness only when the inhibition is lifted: it is like a "suppressed idea in the preconscious". At another level is what he calls the mechanistic threshold, where wholly repressed ideas are still in a state of rebellious activity directed against those in consciousness and succeed in producing indirect effect, e.g., "objectless feelings of oppression". Herbart stated that science knows more than what is actually experienced—the traces of what is stirring and acting "behind the curtains".

One of the most important members of the Herbartian school was the celebrated German psychologist G. T. Fechner, who wrote a noted volume on psychological principles entitled *The Elements of Psychophysics* (1966) towards the end of the nineteenth century when psychology was just beginning to detach itself from philosophy and become a subject of scientific study in its own right. This principle is known to psychologists as "The law of effect", and it is defined by Warren in my ancient *Dictionary of Psychology* as follows: "the law of effect: the principle that a successful or satisfying outcome of a response tends to strengthen its association with the antecendent stimuli, and that an unsuccessful outcome tends to weaken such association" (Warren, 1934). You might think that this is obvious, but sometimes one has to state the obvious and Fechner's law opens up the possibility of studying the development of knowledge and of skills, and, of course, the need for and maintenance of mental representations. Their development can be measured and gradients of learnt behaviour described in terms of stimulus and response. But Fechner also likened the mind to an iceberg, which is nine-tenths under water and whose course is determined not only by the wind, which plays over the surface, but by the currents of the deep.

These various philosophic elements can be shown to have been very important and influential in forming Freud's second, or topographic, theory of mind. But I wish to concentrate on another aspect of these influences, which is summarized by Fechner's quotation from *The Interpretation of Dreams* (Freud, 1899) that *"the scene of action of dreams is different from that of waking ideational life"* (original italics), and later in the same massive book he repeats this remark, saying that this is the only hypothesis that makes the peculiarities of dream life intelligible. In a contemporary letter to Fliess he recounts that in the whole of the world literature on dreams, this is the only sensible remark that he has found.

For the topic under discussion here, this is a crucial statement: Freud seized on the notion that there is *"another theatre in the mind"* that differs from ordinary waking life and that governs the production of dreams and *other* unconscious ideation. You will begin, I hope, to see now why I laid a great deal of stress on my little conjunction "and". This notion of another theatre—in German *der andere Schauplatz*—enables us to create a link between the theatre in everyday life and the internal theatre in each of us, the stage on which we enact and re-enact our psychological dramas. Here is how one distinguished Parisian psychoanalyst describes the internal theatre:

> We all have our neurotic conflicts, our little areas of private folly (at least let us hope so); we are all susceptible to psychosomatic breakdown under stress; and we are all capable of creating perverse fantasies as well as dreaming impossible dreams. [McDougall, 1986, p. 3]

Each of us harbours in our little universe a number of "characters" as McDougall (*ibid.*) explains: these characters are

> parts of ourselves that frequently operate in complete contradiction to one another, causing conflict and mental pain to our conscious selves. for we are relatively unacquainted with these hidden players and their roles. Whether we will it or not, our inner characters are constantly seeking a stage on which to play out their tragedies and comedies. Although we rarely assume responsibility for our secret theatre productions, the producer is seated in our own minds. Moreover, it is this inner world with its repeating repertory that determines most of what happens to us in the external world. [*ibid.*, p. 4]

So here we have a clearly stated psychoanalytic theory about internal theatre—where it is located and of what it consists.

In an Ernest Jones lecture, given a few years ago but unfortunately never published, Peter Brook, the distinguished thinker and twentieth-century man of the theatre, tries to make links between his own professional activity and that of the psychoanalyst. He called the lecture " Does nothing come from nothing?" and begins by saying that: "it doesn't matter if one is talking about theatre or talking about the mind. . . . the same essential and incomprehensible experience [exists] in two completely different types of practical work" (Brook, 1989). After reflecting on the quality in the actor that enables him to identify empathically with a character on the printed page or in the script, he continues:

> Nothing in the theatre has any meaning "before or after" [the performance]. Meaning is "now". An audience comes to the theatre for one reason only, which is to live a certain experience and this experience can only take place at the moment when it is experienced. When this is truly the case, the silence in the theatre changes its density . . . an exact phenomenon occurs. What up until then had been individual experience becomes shared, unified. [*ibid.*, p. 6]

Brook goes on to say that the theatre of tragedy may have a vocation—it can be a healing process. There was a time, he says,

> the time of Greek tragedy, when a whole city could come together and the fragmentation of all the individuals who made up the city would be transformed into a shared intense experience in which self was transcended. For a moment, a life of a completely different nature was tasted and then each person would leave the theatre and go back into their ordinary preoccupations. But a temporary healing of the diseased and fragmented community took place, even if the fragmentation and the conflicts took place again as people left the theatrical space. And the transformation and the taste—and the confidence—it gave could take place again and again whenever the audience came together in the special circumstances of a performance. Society cannot be healed permanently, but temporary healings can redress the balance. [*ibid.*, p. 8]

What I hope you will perceive, as we concentrate on the conjunction *and*, is that there seems to be a striking synergy emerging between psychoanalysis and theatre. Both psychoanalysis and the theatre provide a determinedly neutral but also clearly circumscribed repetitive situation and favour the expression of internal feelings and relationships, which cannot at the beginning be plainly defined but are clearly understood as the products of an interaction between the participants. Furthermore, both psycho-analysis and theatre are staged in a formal and clearly defined way, either in the theatrical space or in the consulting room, and each is insistently repetitive in nature. Neither can be guaranteed to work on every occasion and the audience and the performances can never interact in exactly the same way. Nevertheless, there is some-thing in the repetition and the framework that enables us to get to grips with the internal world in a revolutionary way. I would go so far as to say that the revolutionary drama of fourth century Greece is only superseded by Freud's discovery of the transference and the possibilities of the analytic system at the end of the nineteenth century. Classical Greece staged the questions of life and death and sexuality in dramatic terms, and thus enabled the males of the soci-ety to begin to come to terms with them. (Parenthetically, Didier Anzieu, a distinguished French psychoanalyst who was also Professor of Psychology at Nanterre during the events of May 1968, was very clear that a great deal of what went on then was a staged psychodrama rather than a real revolutionary moment.) On a more intimate scale, Freud's dicoveries, the use of the couch, free associ-ation, and the repetitive nature of an ongoing therapy, have enabled each of us to create an analytic theatre—*den anderen Schauplatz*—to stage and work through our early tragedies and comedies within the analytic framework and to some extent, at least, move towards a better understanding of their determinants. Towards the end of his lecture, Brook remarks that if the theatre has anything unique to offer it is a taste of something that can't be explained and can't be defined, but that can be experienced as a concrete reality.

I want to suggest that there is a demonstrable synergy between psychoanalysis and theatre in that each of them starts with an absolutely bare stage and a situation in which the protagonists can project their internal worlds in any number of ways on to that stage and its properties through their words and actions. Each perfor-mance or session is unique, and yet linked by repetition and a set framework. Each has as a partial goal: the emergence and experi-ence of hitherto untapped and unconscious thoughts and feelings. My emphasis on the "conjunction" concerns the modern link between the two. Psychoanalysis is, at one and the same time, the most formal and the most unstructured of the artistic disciplines. Paintings have frames. Books have authors who are expressing their own feelings and telling their own stories. Both are the work of craftsmen who are trying to communicate on a professional level with an audience.

Their work can be deconstructed by critics using the analytic method in a variety of ways; for example, Elizabeth Wright's text *Psychoanalytic Criticism*, where an excellent academic mind gets to work on these problems. But I am also suggesting that the psychoanalyst has added to all this by providing a key—however imperfect—to the workings of that internal theatre of the protagonists that Joyce McDougall (1986) described and that enables us to suggest an extra dimension to our understanding of the work of art in whatever discipline. By deconstructing a work of art in psychoanalytic terms we can and do deepen and extend our response to the work. We have come to understand that the internal and external theatres are inextricably linked and that to understand one we must learn to understand the other. Francisco Goya, whom Malraux calls the progenitor of Modern Art, gave as the epigraph of his *Caprichos*, "The sleep of reason brings forth monsters", and it has been suggested by Jan Kott (1967) that Hamlet is "the central reflector" for modern life. In fact, this is probably the metaphor for the relationship between psychoanalysis and the theatre that best suits my purpose—that there exists an infinite number of reflections between the inner theatre of phantasy and the external theatre of everyday life, and that examination of plays in these terms will permit us, without interfering with the actual effect of the piece, to increase and deepen our response to the play.

There is one crucial difference, however. The play in the theatre is written by an author who brings to his play both an internal and an external script. We can easily enough understand the reasons why a playwright might wish to tell us the story of the Wars of the Roses or present his view of a hero king. We can also understand that a playwright may wish to amuse and tease us with stories of amorous intrigue or of ways of life we cannot imagine experiencing for ourselves. The author's conscious goals are easily enough described. For example, Oscar Wilde said of *The Importance of Being Earnest* that the philosophy of the play is that we should "treat all trivial things very seriously and all the serious things of life with sincere and studied triviality". What he and his contemporaries were ignorant of was his internal theatre and the themes that were being acted out in the script of the play. Let me repeat here my suggestion that the Freudian revolution has led us to the understanding that the creative work will be a reflection of the internal theatre—the other stage—of the author in terms of which both he and we are probably unaware. We need to know that Earnest was a slang word for homosexual in Wilde's day. Thus, Richard Ellman, in his authoritative biography of Wilde, can say

> *The Importance of Being Earnest* constructs its wonderful parapet over the abyss of the author's disquietude and apprehension. By a desperate strategem Wilde keeps the melancholy of the world at a distance. Erotic passion competes with family ambition, innnocence longs for experience, and experience for innocence. Tears are taboo. A friend said that the play should be like a mosaic. "No," replied the (unconsciously self destructive) Wilde, "it must go like a pistol shot." [Ellman, 1987, p. 224]

In short, without in any way wishing to denigrate the work of the literary historian, the psychoanalytic method—properly used—can suggest a second and additional set of dynamics behind the script that, when appropriately interpreted, increase and deepen our response to the play and to the performance, and lead to the audience response so eloquently described by Peter Brook—which I would myself compare to the result of a good analytic session.

I accept that, holding such a view, I should try to present evidence for my hypothesis. I have therefore chosen a Shakespeare play that I think makes the links clear: *Twelfth Night—or What You Will*. It is appropriate since the play is about so many unconsciously determined themes. Shakespeare felt free to let his colleagues name it after the date on which it was first performed—but they could have called it anything or everything. I have chosen Shakespeare rather than some more modern author with the latest biography, because we know so little about him—see Schoenbaum's *A Documentary Life* (1975). The point about Shakespeare is that we can trace the existence of certain conscious and unconscious themes through the canon that are constantly worked over and re-presented by the writer (see Hildebrand, 1992). This, of course, is where analysis may have something to add to our appreciation of the play. But they have no monopoly of insight and I start with some observations that are to be found in an invaluable text called *Twelfth Night: Directors' Edition* (Billington, 1990)—a discussion between four distinguished directors of the problems of presenting *Twelfth Night* in the theatre. I consider that in many ways the actual problems of staging the play are closer to the psychoanalytic approach than the ideas of the academics, and I shall base much of what I have to say on the remarks of those whose profession it is to bring the printed word to life.

The opening remark that I found noteworthy was made by John Caird in the discussions on the play with Terry Hands, Bill Alexander, and John Barton that Michael Billington has recorded for us. He says, and it is clearly implied that the other directors agree

> in every scene there are words like "death", "decay", "die", "pesti-lence", "hanging" etc.—consistently in every scene there is dark dark imagery, even in the scenes which are famous for being broadly comic. . . . You get at the comedy by going through the darkness of the play. [Billington, 1990]

If Caird is right, we do not have to accept that *Twelfth Night* is prin-cipally a romantic, sunny comedy. I take a more robust, agnostic point of view about the piece in the hope that focusing on the inner theatre will clarify some of the well-known problems with which the piece presents us. I am aware that I am in no way unique in this, for the Introduction to the *Arden Shakespeare* (1975) quotes W. H. Auden as saying of *Twelfth Night* that "Shakespeare was in no mood for comedy, but in a mood of furious aversion to all those puritan-ical illusions which men cherish and by which they lead their lives", although this was perhaps also a projection of his own personal point of view. No less a critic than Frank Kermode (2000) has concluded that the play was a "comedy of identity, set on the borders of wonder and madness", a view that has to be very sympathetic for a psychoanalyst.

I shall also refer to the work of the French psychoanalyst André Green, who, some years ago, wrote a fascinating piece entitled "The double and the absent", which can be found among his collected papers in *On Private Madness* (1972). Green proposes that the task of writing presupposes both a wound and a loss for the writer, so that the work becomes a work of mourning, of which the text is a transformation into a fictitious positivity. Fictitious because, as I have shown in my paper on *The Tempest* (Hildebrand, 1988), the writer in this sense has to constantly rework and reintegrate what has been won and lost (Hildebrand, 1992). With this in mind, I suggest that *Twelfth Night* may be placed in that series of Shakespeare plays which unconsciously involve the reworking and recreation of the internal themes centred on the deaths of, and mourning for, his own father and his son Hamnet (a fraternal twin with a twin sister).

Green (1972) observes that the origin of an idea—the double—may be no more than a fortuitous observation (the germ of the idea with which we are dealing may be very different) and that the final product will be an unconsciously transformed and apparently quite undetermined text (or, of course, a dream). Green demonstrates this through his specimen text—Henry James' novel *The Ambassadors*—where he demonstrates how a psychological relationship may develop a life of its own on the page. Green is saying that the text resembles the manifest content of a dream that needs to be interpreted to understand the latent unconscious anxieties behind it. Indeed, I think that one could go further and say that the text as it develops becomes like a series of dreams that we may dream on the same night in order to try and resolve some specific anxiety. In my experience, such a series most often represents a number of attempts to come to terms with the dreamer's problem. Unfortunately, the latent content of a creative work is not the same as a series of dreams, since the author is not on our couch and we must project our own phantasy on to both the author and the text in order to try to evoke a meaning that we can accept and that will be convincing to others. For Green, the text is a potential space in which we can find what we want and need in terms of our own and others' inner worlds. But it also has the potentiality to reverberate for us with certain universal symbolisms, whatever the goal for which the personal internal world of the writer might have used this space. It is here that Green brings in his notion of the "Absent", which, like the phantasy latently underlying a dream, like the (non-existent and therefore profoundly powerful) female phallus of Lacan's brilliant gloss on *The Purloined Letter* (1988), is endowed by us with power without our being necessarily aware of what we are doing.

Is there, then, from a psychoanalytic viewpoint, an "absent" in *Twelfth Night*? I suggest there is indeed one. It seems to me that the whole play centres around the fantasy of the primal scene, both the power of the primal phantasy and our fear of its presentation together with a dramatization of the Oedipus complex as seen from a child's point of view. Here, I would follow the account of phantasy and the origins of sexuality suggested by Laplanche and Pontalis in *The Language of Psychoanalysis* (1973). Speaking of *primal phantasies*, they say,

> If we consider the themes which can be recognised in primal phantasies, the striking thing is that they have one thing in common: they are all related to the *origins*. Like collective myths they claim to provide a representation of and a "solution" to whatever constitutes a major enigma for the child. Whatever appears to the subject as a reality of such a type as to require and explanation or "theory", these phantasies dramatize into the primal moment or original point of departure of a history. ["If music be the food of Love, play on / Give me excess of it".] In the "primal scene", it is the origin of the subject that is represented; in seduction phantasies, it is the origin or emergence of sexuality: in castration phantasies, the origin of the distinction between the sexes. [*ibid.*, p. 332]

For Laplanche and Pontalis, the universitality of these structures (primal phantasies) needs, as I have just suggested, to be related to the universality that Freud accords to the Oedipus complex, *viz*:

> The content of the sexual life of infancy consists in auto-erotic activity on the part of the dominant sexual components, in traces of object love, and in the formation of that complex which deserves to be called *the nuclear complex of the neuroses* [Freud's italics]. . . . The uniformity of the content of the sexual life of children, together with the unvarying character of the modifying tendencies which are later brought to bear upon it, will easily account for the constant sameness which as a rule characterizes the phantasies which are constructed around the period of childhood, irrespective of how greatly or how little real experiences have contributed to them. It is entirely characteristic of the nuclear complex of infancy that the child's father should be assigned the part of a sexual opponent and

of an interferer with auto-erotic sexual activities: and real events are usually to a large extent responsible for bringing this about. [Freud, 1909d]

I now suggest that Olivia's virginity and its potential destruction through the primal scene provide the unconscious dynamic of *Twelfth Night* in the same way that Susanna's newly awakened sexuality provides the dynamic underlying the plot of *The Marriage of Figaro*. But why do we have the dance of deception and self-deception in *Twelfth Night*? What is going on between Olivia, Orsino, and Viola? Let me remind you of Fechner's aphorism "the scene of action of dreams is different from that of waking ideational life". It takes place—please mark the phrase well, as did Freud—in *einem anderen Schauplatz*, which in the play in question Shakespeare names Illyria (or illusion). The phrase is conventionally translated as "another scene", but *la scene* in French is, of course, "the stage". So, when referring to this notion, I have preferred to speak of "another theatre". This change of location of mental energy is taken up and expanded in the essay on "The unconscious" (Freud, 1915e), where Freud categorically states "Consciousness makes each of us aware of his own states of mind: that other people too possess a consciousness is an inference which we draw from their behaviour" (p. 169). From this argument he goes on to derive the topological theory of the unconscious in order to account for repression and the existence of differing grades of mental activity. And we all ascribe ideas, wishes, and desires to others, just as others inscribe their desires in us. Freud says,

> it may happen that an affective or emotional impulse is perceived but misconstrued. Owing to the repression of its proper representative it has been forced to become connected with another idea, and is now regarded by consciousness as the manifestation of that idea. [*ibid.*, p. 177]

I suggest that in a good theatrical performance the situation allows us to double our response to the play and the performers and creates—sometimes—that extraordinary theatrical experience of which Peter Brook spoke.

Let me now try to apply these notions that I have briefly sketched in to *Twelfth Night*, and we find that we have some interesting inferences that we can draw. For the aristocrats in the play, I suggest that each can at first discover his own desire through his or her attribution of his feelings to and through another, so that the feelings find their overt and forceful expression literally "in another theatre". So, Orsino says in the first scene,

ORSINO: O, when mine eyes did see Olivia first,
            Methought she purg'd the air of pestilence;
            That instant was I turned into a hart,
            And my desires, like fell and cruel hounds,
            E'er since pursue me. (1.1: 18–23)

and at the end of the scene, after Valentine has told him of Olivia's vow of seven years mourning and chastity.

ORSINO: O, she that hath a heart of that fine frame
            To pay this debt of love but to a brother,
            How will she love, when the rich golden shaft
            Hath killed the flock of all affections else
            That live in her; when the liver, brain and heart,
            These sovereign thrones, are all supplied and filled
            Her sweet perfections with one self king!
            Away before me to sweet beds of flowers
            Love thoughts lie rich when canopied with bowers.
            (1.1: 32–41)

Olivia thus becomes the person through whom Orsino can find his sexual desire in the other theatre that he creates by his investment in her: yet Olivia is apparently safe because as far as both he and she are concerned she is conveniently locked into her Oedipal mourning for her dead father and brother and he can invest her with his erotic romantic idealization in complete safety.

Viola, too, is locked into mourning for Sebastian, the "drowned" twin. John Barton says, "I went for the feeling of fairy tale and dream and strangeness and of her coming out of the sea like Aphrodite coming out of the waves of mist, so that she didn't quite know where she was. I said that the most important of her lines in this scene was 'What country, friends, is this?'" Surely implicitly, then, we are talking of a birth phantasy and Viola's loss of her twin in the course of the birth. Parenthetically, many people in analysis have a phantasy of having had a twin who has died *in utero* and, as we now know from the studies on *in vitro* fertilization, this may often have been true. So, a second "absent" we are concerned with is both a phantasy about birth and about gender identity. Viola has lost her twin and instead of being therefore sure of her own gender identity in contrast with Sebastian, she has to decide on her own identity first within the terms of the twinship, and its secondary reflection in the outer world.

Viola will discover that Orsino is infatuated with Olivia, who is in mourning for her father and brother, as the Captain reports to her, and Viola muses.

VIOLA: Oh that I served that lady
          And might not be delivered to the world
          Till I had made mine own occasion mellow,
          What my estate is. (1.2: 42–46)

So Viola will experimentally don a boy's disguise in order to serve Orsino. She, too, "can sing, / and speak to him in many sorts of music" (1.2: 57–58). Within the disguise she can mourn Sebastian, without actual sexual involvement with another man, by becoming her male twin until such time as she, too, has completed the task of mourning.

Of course, things do not quite work out as they hope. Orsino doubles the effect of the investment in phantasy by his immediate intimacy with Viola.

ORSINO: Thou knowest no less but all: I have unclasped
          To thee the book even of my secret soul. (1.4: 15–16)

In terms of Freud's papers on the psychology of love (1933a), Orsino is able to displace on to Viola (in the creative writer's hands here the boy–girl becomes the acceptable surrogate for the Freudian debased woman with whom one can experience ideas and feelings that have to be kept from the idealized lover) the split-off internal world of "sexual" phantasy that he cannot reveal to Olivia, the idealized love object. Olivia, for her part, is, of course, well aware of the unreality of his infatuation, as when, in reply to Viola's praise of her on behalf of Orsino, she categorizes herself thus:

OLIVIA: How does he love me?
VIOLA: With adorations, fertile tears,
          With groans that thunder love, with sighs of fire.

OLIVIA: Your lord does know my mind, I cannot love him.
           (1.5: 264–267)

Indeed, Olivia is much more hard-headed than one might
suppose.

OLIVIA: Oh sir I will not be so hard-hearted. I shall give out
           divers schedules of my beauty. It shall be inventoried
           and every particle and utensil labelled to my will, as,
           item, two lips, indifferent red; item, two grey eyes, with
           lids to them; item, one neck, one chin, and so forth.
           Were you sent hither to praise me?" (1.5: 252–258)

Olivia, then, can be extremely practical. She seems perfectly well
aware that Orsino is only deceiving himself about her and that he
is as much or more in love with romantic love as he is with her. That
she is desirable is clear to her and that she is looking for some
acceptable way in which she can work out her own desires seems
important to her. What she plainly does not want to do is to give
way to Orsino's phantasy and become a player in his theatre.

Viola too, as in the willow cabin speech, can best discover her
desire for Orsino in a disguised way—she has described herself as
"his eunuch"—without the object of her love being aware of it.
Consider, please, the following dialogue between Olivia and Viola.

VIOLA: If I did love you in my master's flame,
           with such a suffering, such a deadly life,
           In your denial I would find no sense,
           I would not understand it.
OLIVIA: Why what would you?
VIOLA: Make me a willow cabin at your gate,
           And call upon my soul within the house;
           Write loyal cantons of contemned love,
           And sing them loud even in the dead of night;
           Halloo your name to the reverberate hills,
           And make the babbling gossip of the air
           Cry out Olivia! O, you should not rest
           Between the elements of air and earth,
           But you should pity me"
OLIVIA: You might do much.
           What is your parentage?" (1.5: 275–287)

Viola's courtship of Olivia on behalf of Orsino and Olivia's immediate response to Viola–Cesario, who is clearly identifed as being between boy and man, enables both girls to express desire in a non-masculine and therefore non-frightening way, so that the love they are talking about can be divorced from physical sexuality— though whether the joke is on the players or the audience, given the fact that both roles were taken by boys disguised as girls, I am not really sure. What Jan Kott (1967) has called the reflector in Shakespeare, the mirroring of several layers each mutually reflecting, is once again in evidence here. Please note the exchange between Olivia and Viola in Act Three, Scene One.

OLIVIA: . . . I prithee tell me what thou think'st of me
VIOLA: That you do think you are not what you are.
OLIVIA: If I think so, I think the same of you.
VIOLA: Then think you right; I am not what I am.
OLIVIA: I would you were as I would have you be. (3.1: 142–149)

I think that that exchange clearly proves my point.

So, all three aristocratic protagonists are caught up in the desires of the other, and use the other theatre in themselves to distance themselves from the realities of life and, of course, of sexuality. The force of the play lies precisely in this fact; that each achieves power solely through the other's desire and at the cost of his or her own desire. We get the Romance; but at one remove from everyday life. That's what the audience wills and what the author is providing them with, but at a cost. Sir Toby has surely got it right when he says, "What a plague means my niece to take the death of her brother thus? I am sure care's an enemy to life" (1.3: 2–3).

And, of course, life goes on in a much more real way with the fatuities of Malvolio and the plots of Maria and her cohorts. What is so strong here is that Shakespeare is doubling the same Freudian game, but using Malvolio and the clowns at the level of comedy and cruel mockery rather than high romance.

Malvolio's desire is for self advancement and for power and position as well as the possession of Olivia's person, her dowry, and her wealth. It is easy to see how Sir Toby and the others may mock this trait for us, and drive him close to madness, while we can laugh at his discomfiture. Yet I feel that the whole Malvolio sub-plot, which in some ways seems so alien to the romantic elements of the play, can be assimilated to the argument I have been putting forward.

As well as the triangle of Orsino–Olivia–Viola, with their intersecting phantasies, there are other triangles in the play. One is Malvolio–Olivia–Toby, which is concerned with more pragmatic matters than romantic love. We are looking at an Elizabethan household and the stakes are substantial. Possession of Olivia's body means also possession of her dowry and her family goods. Indeed, the whole question of marriage is central to the other triangle of Maria–Toby–Olivia as well. I suggest that Shakespeare actually works this out on several levels throughout the play—both from Viola's first remark about Orsino—"he was a bachelor, then"—to the final resolution. The third absent in the sense of Green's hypotheses is the person of the father, since Olivia's father is dead and so is Viola's. But who is acting as a surrogate father in the household? Olivia's steward, Malvolio. On his first appearance, when Olivia is playing word games with Feste, he makes it plain that he disapproves of the clown,

MALVOLIO: I marvel that your ladyship takes delight in such a barren rascal: I saw him put down the other day with an ordinary fool that has no more brain than a stone. (1.5: 75–78)

and, as he lets us know in the carousal scene, he, whatever anyone else in the house may think, is certainly a respecter of place, persons, and time—and expects everyone else to respect him and what he stands for. It is this self importance for which Sir Toby attacks him when Malvolio tells him that Olivia threatens to send him away because of the noise and the nuisance of his drunken singing.

SIR TOBY: . . . Art any more than a steward? Does thou think that because thou art virtuous, there shall be no more cakes and ale? (2.3: 106–108)

Malvolio's pretensions to Olivia's hand have been understood by Maria, who is nothing if not street-smart, and very much on the lookout for a husband even if he is a sot like Sir Toby, and what we get now is the delicious comedy of taking Malvolio down several pegs. In the box-tree scene, we are allowed to share his day-dreams of being Olivia's husband and how he will take over the estate, Olivia's person, and put Sir Toby and Sir Andrew in their places— a fantasy of being the Master of the House, in reality. The point here is that the plot revolves around making Malvolio look ridiculous— and, in my view, behind the comedy, which although we all know it by heart, seems always to succeed when the play is well acted and Malvolio has a real presence and real substance at the beginning— there is a latent element that, as far as I know, no one has pointed out so far: *viz.*, that what we are getting is the mockery that a group of children indulge in when faced with adults who seek to impose standards on them. The joke that is played on Malvolio is at first no more than a schoolboy jape, so that he is gulled by Maria's letter— The Father, or at least the man who is trying to become the Father and take on that role, is mocked by the children who do not wish to accept his authority. I am reminded of nothing so much as an unsuccessful prep school teacher who cannot keep order and who is continually persecuted by a group of small boys. But, like small boys, they over-egg the pudding—Bill Alexander in the directors' discussions says,

> There is tremendous cruelty in what they do to Malvolio. I don't think that you can avoid that. If you try to, you make the pain and the love and the balance of humour in the play rather pointless— the play develops a soft centre. The comedy becomes a meaningless game if it's just a jolly comeuppance for Malvolio; it's not, it's viciously cruel what they do. [Billington, 1990]

So perhaps it's no wonder that Malvolio is driven into such a fury that Olivia decides that he has gone mad and orders him locked up.

In the meantime the congruent working out of the romance continues. Olivia falls in love in her turn with Cesario.

OLIVIA: Cesario, by the roses of the spring,
            By maidhood, honour, truth, and everything,
            I love thee so that, maugre all my pride,
            Nor wit nor reason can my passion hide. (3.1: 149–153)

I don't know who said that falling in love is a mild form of psychosis, but the romantic declarations of *Twelfth Night* would seem to support the suggestion, which is perhaps not so true of Viola, who is acutely aware of her infatuation with Orsino but only indirectly tells him of her desire. Here the comedy turns on the gender mix-up and the ways in which Viola can both declare her feelings and at the same time conceal them. Listen while Orsino orates about his love.

ORSINO: . . . Mine is all as hungry as the sea;
           and can digest as much. Make no compare
           Between that love a woman can bear me
           And that I owe Olivia.
VIOLA: Ay, but I know—
ORSINO: What doest thou know?
VIOLA: Too well what love women to men may owe.
           In faith, they are as true of heart as we.
           My father had a daughter loved a man
           As it might be, perhaps, were I a woman
           I should your lordship.
ORSINO: And what's her history?
VIOLA: A blank my lord: she never told her love,
           But let concealment like a worm in the bud
           Feed on her damask cheek: she pined in thought,
           And with a green and yellow melancholy
           She sat like Patience on a monument,
           Smiling at grief. Was not this love indeed?
           We men may say more, swear more, but indeed,
           Our shows are more than will: for still we prove
           Much in our vows, but little in our love.
ORSINO: But died thy sister of her love, my boy?
VIOLA: I am all the daughters of my father's house,
           And all the brothers too: and yet I know not.
           (2.4: 102—124)

Viola has other problems to deal with in her struggle with the question of gender identity and castration anxiety—the duel to which she is challenged by Sir Andrew being not the least since it threatens to expose her as a man without a true weapon. But Sebastian's arrival on the scene and his thrashing of Sir Andrew and Sir Toby will rescue her and restore the lovers to some sort of equanimity or at least to the unwinding of the plot.

In the meantime we have the extraordinary Sir Topas scene, which the directors say no one quite understands. Until now, I have said nothing about Feste, the clown, but I regard him as being in many ways the playwright's commentator on the whole piece. I think those who feel that he should be in the Third Age, and thus past the passions of the younger characters, must be right, and it is interesting that he is the only character in the whole play who is involved with everyone. Just as Malvolio is the despised and insulted father, Feste represents the ironic, wordly-wise, disguised father who has seen it all before. He spends his time gently outwitting and taking the aristocrats down a peg, while ironically observing the turmoil of Olivia's household. He is the reasonable man who does not wish to be on bad terms with anyone providing that they are pleasant to him and tip him generously. It is only the upwardly mobile middle-class Malvolio, who tells him that he's a rotten clown, who really provokes him; perhaps it is for that reason that he agrees to become Sir Topas—he certainly is not involved in the letter scene—such japes are rather beneath him.

What he does do is enjoy a very savage revenge on Malvolio: as Sir Topas, he first refuses to believe that Malvolio is not mad but sane, he catechizes him and mocks his responses and finally leaves him in despair. He then plays the doubling game by reappearing moments later as himself singing "Tell me how my lady does—she loves another" and once again we get the ironic dialogue of doubling or, as one might say in an analytic supervision, splitting.

MALVOLIO: Good fool, as ever thou wilt deserve well at my hand, help me to a candle and pen and ink and paper: as I am a gentleman, I will live to be thankful to thee for it.
FESTE: Master Malvolio?
MALVOLIO: Ay good fool.
FESTE: Alas sir, how fell you beside your five wits?
MALVOLIO: Fool, there never was man so notoriously abused: I am as well in my wits, fool, as thou art.
FESTE: But as well? Then you are mad indeed, if you be no better in your wits than a fool. (4.2: 85–94)

The comedy of each character doubling the other is being played out yet again in this sadistic teasing, which Malvolio has brought upon himself with his pride and his ambition. The fool tells the sane man that he is mad so that reality and madness interweave in this scene as they do all through the play. Perhaps I should have borrowed the title of Donald Winnicott's last book, *Playing and Reality*, for the title of this piece. But in the same way as, in Winnicott's view, mothers have to be able to hold their hatred and their sadism within themselves for their children to grow optimally, so we have the situation of the cruelty of the gulling of Malvolio as the ground against which the marvellous poetry of the romantic scenes can evolve.

The title that I originally chose for the chapter was "The wind and the rain". I felt that the last Act, with its confrontation of the various inner worlds of the characters, represented the proposal by the playwright to the audience that, just as later in *The Tempest*, illusion will not work or the other theatre resolve our problems of love and gender identity. As Orsino says when confronted with Sebastian and Viola (who, incidentally, do not need to be played by twin actors—the identity, like beauty, is in the eye of the beholder),

ORSINO: One face, one voice, one habit and two persons
              A natural perspective that is and is not. (5.1: 216–218)

Sir Toby marries Maria, a real forced marriage, Malvolio is brought in to be questioned, and, on a more romantic level, the gentry pair off. Feste's speech here explains it all.

FESTE: Why, "Some are born great, some achieve greatness,
         and some have greatness thrown upon them." I was
         one, sir, in this interlude, one Sir Topas, sir, but that's
         all one. "By the lord, fool, I am not mad"—but do you
         remember, "Madam, why laugh you at such a barren
         rascal, an you smile not, he's gagged"—and thus the
         whirligig of time brings in his revenges.

Malvolio, who has no charity, replies "I'll be revenged on the whole pack of you" (5.1 370–377) and exits in a furious rage, so that the Father substitute is finally defeated and discarded.

Orsino bids them pacify him, he and the others depart, and Feste sings his little song about disillusionment—the romantic passions we have seen are but illusions and no more, and reality is both sadder and less romantic than the writer has proposed. The song is a commentary on the whole romantic delightful nonsense we have seen *and* tells us that we should not take it as anything else.

FESTE: When that I was a little tiny boy,
          With hey, ho, the wind and the rain,
          A foolish thing was but a toy,
          For the rain it raineth every day

          But when I came to man's estate,
          With hey, ho, the wind and the rain,
          'Gainst knaves and thieves men shut their gate,
          For the rain it raineth every day

          But when I came, alas, to wive,
          With hey, ho, the wind and the rain
          By swaggering could I never thrive
          For the rain it raineth every day

          But when I came unto my beds,
          With hey, ho, the wind and the rain,
          With tosspots still had drunken heads,
          For the rain it raineth every day

          A great while ago the world begun
          With hey, ho, the wind and the rain,
          But that's all one, our play is done,
          And we'll strive to please you every day. (5.1: 389–409)

I have spoken of my notion that the whole play revolves around Olivia's dowry, both material and sexual, and Orsino makes the point quite clear in Act 5.1: "should I not . . . kill what I love" He will kill Cesario–Viola in order to achieve final mastery over Olivia.. The primal scene is perhaps a primal scream, and we have to recognize the intense rage that sits behind all the romantic goings-on. After the extraordinary Sir Topas scene, which seems much like the return of the repressed, the rage, of course, is echoed by Malvolio when he makes his final exit demanding revenge. The audience tends to laugh at this speech—after all we can but laugh at what we most fear. Green (1972) says "Ghost means death. And absence means potential death. What then does this pleasure [of watching the play] have to do with death?" His answer, which will do well enough for my purposes today, is that we each of us create a potential space—as the audience—within which in our own minds we will echo the phantasy and each of us constantly rework it on our own personal terms. When, finally, Sebastian's entry breaks up the game on both levels, the plot can be wound up. Olivia can marry a man who is not after her wealth, Viola can find her true gender identity, the Duke can come to life in a real relationship, and a real primal scene can be allowed. The father is defeated and at the same time the law of the father resumes its place. Even Malvolio can be restored, if not to his former pomp, at least to the world.

This is where the true link between psychoanalysis and theatre may be found. Like the play, I have no Epilogue—but I would point out that there is no Shakespearean Epilogue that makes my point more powerfully than Feste's song in *Twelfth Night*.

References

Billington, M. (Ed.) (1990). *Twelfth Night: Directors' Edition*. Nick Hearn.

Brook, P. (1989). Does nothing come of nothing? Ernest Jones Lecture.

Ellman, R. (1987). *Oscar Wilde*. New York: Random House Value.

Fechner, G. T. (1966). *Elements of Psychophysics. Volume I*. New York: Holt, Rinehart and Winston.

Freud, S. (1899). *The Interpretation of Dreams. S.E.*, 5. London: Hogarth.

Freud, S. (1909d). Two case histories: Little Hans and the Rat Man. Notes on a case of obsessional neurosis. *S.E.*, 10: 200–220. London: Hogarth.

Freud, S. (1915e). The unconscious: various meanings of "the unconscious"—a topographical view. *S.E.*, 14. London: Hogarth.

Freud, S. (1933a). *New Introductory Lectures on Psycho-Analysis. Femininity. S.E.*, 112–136. London: Hogarth.

Green, A. (1972). *On Private Madness*. London: Hogarth.

Hildebrand, H. P. (1988). The other side of the wall. A psychoanalytical study of creativity in later life. *International Review of Psychoanalysis*, 15: 353–364.

Jones, E. (1980). *Sigmund Freud*. London: Hogarth.

Kermode, F. (2000). *Shakespeare's Language*. London: Allen Lane.

Kott, J. (1967). *Shakespeare Our Contemporary*. London: Methuen.

Lacan, J. (1988). Seminar on "The Purloined Letter". In: J. P. Muller & W. J. Richardson (Eds.), J. Mehlman (Trans.), Chicago: Johns Hopkins University Press.

Laplanche, J., & Pontalis, J.-B. (1973). *The Language of Psychoanalysis*. London: Hogarth.

McDougall, J. (1986). *Theatres of the Mind: Illusion and Truth on the Analytic Stage*. London: Free Association.

Shakespeare, W. *The Arden Shakespeare: Complete Works*. Arden.

Schoenbaum, S. (1975). *William Shakespeare: A Documentary Life*. New York: Oxford University Press.

Warren, H. (Ed.) (1934). *Dictionary of Psychology*. New York: Houghton Mifflin.

Wright, E. (1984). *Psychoanalytic Criticism: Theory in Practice*. London: Methuen.

CHAPTER TWO

Grief, loss, and creativity: whither the Phoenix?

Gerald Wooster and Peter Buckroyd

The central idea in this chapter is that out of loss can come the creative impulse. Moreover, attending to the vicissitudes of the affective responses to loss may help us to distinguish between the destructive and more creative sequelae of loss. Loss in real and metaphorical ways, as we know, provokes anger, guilt, and sadness. The grief of loss is a complex state of mind with different lengths of duration, and in each individual shows different mixes of other constituent affects, such as anger, guilt, shame, mixed with envy and jealousy as well as frequently accompanying depression with varying degrees of somatic disruptions. Each person has a different threshold of defences against depression, among which the manic defence is the most characteristic.

Since loss plays so great a part in creativity, it is important first to consider depressive response to loss and its characteristic defence by examining some psychoanalytic ideas that provide a framework for thinking about creativity. We shall go on to consider one of the most comprehensive descriptions of the common factors in creativity: Rothenberg's *The Emerging Goddess* (1979). We shall then consider the group as a crucible in which grief, loss, and creativity can be expressed in different ways. Last, we shall examine the

writer who is perhaps the most striking exemplar of all these experiences, Shakespeare, whose middle period play *All's Well That Ends
Well* binds together grief, loss, and creativity, both in its own
content and in the circumstances surrounding its composition and
context.

Research work, particularly by Lewis and Bourne, has shown
how difficult it is approaching or around the time of birth for
normal mourning processes to take place. The denial and confusion
involved in accepting minus one at the time of creating plus one—
a situation shared by others in the powerful emotional field
surrounding the mother at birth—has been further highlighted by
the same researchers' important work on stillbirths, which demonstrates the hidden resistances that appear to take place both to
mourning and to its subsequent remembering and recording in
history. It might be easier to accept a continuation of nought rather
than explore the painful status of the minus one, particularly since
it is so easy for there to be little conscious noting of the potential
plus one, since the baby that represents the potential for new life is
out of sight in the womb. This research work illustrates how difficult it is to sort out the emotional complexities of situations where
births and deaths are found in close proximity.

There may be something of the same difficulty for those faced
with another kind of loss: a missing person. The ambiguity of loss
makes it difficult for the subject to know where he is in relation to
the emotional task in hand. This can be seen dramatically in Arthur
Miller's first theatrical creative hit, *All My Sons*, in which a family
loses one of two sons in the Second World War. The denial of the
depressive reality that afflicted the mother of the missing son eventually affects her ability to cope with her husband's death as well
as that of her dead son (minus two rather than just minus one).

It is important when considering such losses to remind
ourselves of modern ways of handling grief that recognize the
importance of seeing the dead person or baby. The actuality of
death needs to be marked with the senses so that any ambiguity
concerning its presence can be squashed.

The creative artist uses this area of ambiguity. A death may be
represented straight in a tragedy, but, even if it happened in real
life, can also be used in a comic solution, so that a denial mechan-
ism is used in a manic way to imagine what might have been. In

such a way the creative artist can use the area of ambiguity surrounding death to deny the loss of the loved one. This perhaps most obviously underpinned Shakespeare's creation of the Romance group of plays at the end of his career. Peter Hildebrand has written a very interesting paper demonstrating the similarity of the dynamic structures of *Hamlet* and *The Tempest*, where in *The Tempest* everybody is preserved for its happy ending, a comic denouement that contrasts vividly with the carnage at the end of *Hamlet*. However, Shakespeare's creative use of the manic fantasy in comedy found expression much earlier in his career.

Shakespeare is particularly interested to explore in his work the different ways in which two can become one and one can become two. Sometimes he uses his characters as mirrors of each other; at other times one self becomes two characters. In this way one can play two and two can play one. The simplest example of this is a pun: the meaning is true in two different ways at the same time. Also, Freud records his friend Jekles as having suggested that one should see Macbeth and Lady Macbeth as two aspects of one character (1916, p. 323). Throughout his career, Shakespeare's plays reflect births and losses in his own life, private and public. Shakespeare divides and doubles at will and can encourage us in turn to follow his creative example.

An individual can also carry disparate family histories within him or her, so that in some respects he or she becomes two. This is particularly germane when considering the subsequent lives of children born in the shadow of another's death. Such children carry both positives and negatives from their situation as they grow up: a study of people's first names is often revealing. I have felt in my own history-taking that a powerful idealization or a black sheep projective identification from the previous generation may affect the course of a person's life; this especially occurs when people reach the age that their parents were when they or their next sibling was born. It may be important for us as psychotherapists to pick up the interwoven and disparate sides of themselves that our patients may be showing. The split may represent introjecting warring parents. If abuse or trauma intervenes, an early introject of an important figure may exist in isolation, however internally digested, which may suddenly erupt. Multiple personality phenomena are often underpinned by severe degrees of this experience.

There are times, however, when family members may kindle afresh the past family figure whom the individual is carrying within him or herself.

This phenomenon of the individual's carrying of a past family history was clarified for me by Avril Earnshaw, an Australian psychotherapist who introduced me to ideas about such critical dates in people's lives. She was surprised to find in a small series that mothers often gave birth to an autistic child at the age when their own mother had had a stillbirth. We also know that children of especial promise have been born following the death of previous siblings; Shakespeare himself was one of these. It is interesting that both Beethoven and van Gogh were born a year to the day after a previous sibling's death.

Attending to the manic-depressive bipolarity is important in studying the creative impulse. Kay Jamison's study of a group of very creative artists (Jamison, 1989) showed that there was a high percentage among them of manic-depressives, particularly among poets. Robert Lowell was one of her examples. We may also consider the nature of creativity by examining this particular manic-depressive split in the underlying character structure of creative patients. In our opinion, such people are characterized by a split in their subjective sense of time between periods of despair, which represents a travesty of common depressive reality, and periods of denial, the manic state that sees the future suffused with false hope and that equally loses touch with the hard ground of depressive reality. These polarities are so disconnected that each is felt infinitely, with no experience of the other pole. Each person has his own bedrock of depressive reality that his consciousness is trying to escape. This desire to escape is extraordinarily infectious to those around, so that it becomes even more important to anchor any outburst of manic excitement to its appropriate depressive core. Each unintegrated swing of the pendulum in time makes for a vicious circle, a tradition laid down like this: depressive failure which cannot be stayed with is followed by the even greater need to turn again to the manic defence. The capacity for self-destruction in such people is high, shown not just by the high suicide rate but also by their personal relationships and the fate of their creative endeavours. They need help in sorting out what is of value in their own depressive loss and in appreciating true hope and the reparative capacity that can be extracted from their manic swing. It is my belief that aspects of the bi-polar dynamic exist sub-clinically in many never-diagnosed manic-depressives. It was said of Shake-speare's most manic–depressive character, Timon of Athens, that "the middle of humanity thou never knewest but the extremity of both ends" (Shakespeare, 1967, *Timon of Athens*, 4.3: 300–301).

So, we have two clinical tasks to keep in mind in the manage-ment of the manic. One is that we must consistently hold for them the anchor of their specific depressive reality, however unpleasant. The other is that we must value, and sometimes save from destruc-tive punishment, the core of their creativity.

During my training at the Psychotherapy Department of the Maudsley Hospital, Henri Rey emphasized the importance of remembering the gender stereotypes represented in the two poles of the manic depressives: first, the male, whose man-ic penis is shooting off in different directions but always away from the woman, and second the woman, who in her depression is either left empty with herself on her own, or left holding the baby, screaming, and entirely without the man's help. Bringing these two halves together in mutually supportive complementary and creative inter-course needs to occur both inter-psychically (sexual intercourse representing one plus one that may equal three) and intra-psychi-cally (a half plus a half equals one whole or entire), creating a bridg-ing middle ground by bringing the two halves of the psyche together.

In our therapeutic stance, we must watch out for the manic impulse, which may manifest itself in several different ways, either in anticipation of death, in a glorification of dying, including the very act itself, or in a manic grandiosity afforded to those who have died. It is also possible to see how a partisan patriotism may take over this experience of death, particularly when we are considering the political sphere. Both in our study of politics and in our work with psychotic patients, we need to see where manic denial mech-anisms start up in tandem with projective mechanisms in an infla-tionary paranoid grandiosity.

The creative artist may not always remember the depression that lies behind the creative response. If he does not, he can be in danger of a takeover by somebody who wants to use manic infla-tion to build an empire for his own purposes. Such empires can be in both the real world and the world of entertainment. Alexander, Napoleon, Hitler, and Milosevic have all had their particular manic dream of political empire. We have also seen the interesting phenomenon of the USA in our generation building up an empire of entertainment and film in Hollywood that not only represented the fantasy of the American Dream but, through the glorification of its B movie star (Reagan), provided a model of supposedly rational government.

We have found the most gripping and relevant book on the creative process to be that with the phoenix-like title, *The Emerging Goddess*. It was written by a psychoanalyst, Albert Rothenberg, who as a research professor at Yale with a National Institute of Mental Health (NIMH) grant, interviewed in dynamic depth a great number and range of creative people in the arts, sciences, and other fields over a period of fifteen years. Giving exciting examples from these different fields, he details what he believes to be the common factors that make for intense creativity. He finds that it is necessary for some characteristics of the dream or of dream processes to be present in the consciously controlled thoughts of the creative artist, and he singles out two specific characteristics of such thought.

The first characteristic is an atemporal use of opposites that he calls Janusian thinking, after the Roman god who looked in two opposite directions at the same time. The idea is to bridge a paradox, as it were, by superimposing two or more opposite or antithetical ideas, images, or concepts simultaneously. It involves giving equal weight to both components, often across different times and from different parts of the mind. It involves primary process thinking and the use of what Matte Blanco (1975) calls symmetrical logic.

The second process, called homospatial thinking, consists of superimposing two or more discrete entities occupying the same space, a conception which allows a new identity to be articulated. Although most often visual, the process may involve any of the other sensory modalities. It involves the superimposition of whole entities rather than the consideration of parts side by side. It is a type of spatial abstraction taken from nature, an integration of Janusian processes. One of its chief functions is to produce creative metaphors. It can bring concepts and precepts together in words and/or images. It can bring together, for instance, subject and object or different affective responses such as sex and aggression, reality and myth, or past image and present image. All of these possibilities, drawn from our knowledge of the mind as exemplified in dreams, can be performed in directed consciousness by the creative person. These two processes, then, can be harnessed by the creator—the one, Janusian thinking, allowing one to become two, and the other, homospatial thinking, for two to become one. Matte Blanco's valuable description of bi-logic may also help us to understand the workings of creativity, although Rothenberg appears not to be familiar with Matte Blanco's work.

There are two obvious reasons for singling out a dramatist and a play to exemplify this paper's theme. The first has to do with the characteristics of the event of theatre going. Whereas many creative activities are essentially solitary, merely drawing on corporate experience, the theatre is a medium where there is, by its very nature, a corporate involvement in the artistic process. The audience is aware not only of the actors but also of the other audience members, and these together create a moment and a series of moments in which spoken and unspoken communications combine to have a complex effect, both individual and corporate. A performance has a series of triangles built into it, and it therefore shares many similar creative potentialities to those of a group, which may not be available, or may be available in a different way, in one to one experiences.

In introducing Shakespeare, we are becoming more and more conscious of how extraordinary his experience was to be the leader of a group of players over a period of at least eighteen years with only minimal and gradual changes of personnel. It has not been sufficiently clearly pointed out that the central core of Shakespeare's players shared bereavements in losing their original leaders. The Earl of Leicester's play troop, Leicester's Men, was taken over on his death in 1588 by Ferdinando, Lord Strange. He in turn became Earl of Derby in 1593 but died the following year. Then the troop re-formed under the name of the Countess of Derby's Players, and then quickly became the Lord Chamberlain's Players, late in 1594. The Earl of Derby's death in 1594, however, was by no means the only one. During the period from 1592 to 1594 four of the Elizabethan poet-dramatists—Greene, Watson, Marlowe, Kyd—all died, in addition to the players' leader and patron, Lord Strange. It would be hard to imagine a more creative group, as they turned their joint personal experience of loss into the performances of a string of masterpieces that mark the high point of British drama in the Elizabethan, or indeed any, period.

The play by Shakespeare that we want to consider in some detail in relationship to this theme of grief, loss, and creativity is one of those rather infrequently played, *All's Well That Ends Well*. It picks up themes, particularly from earlier plays about eight to ten years before it, but its approximate date of composition of 1601–1602 would link it to Shakespeare's father's own death in 1601, and also to the recent bereavement of his patroness, the Countess of Pembroke, and her son William, who had just lost husband and father. In this way it catches the two bereaved Williams (Shakespeare himself and William Herbert, who have both lost their fathers).

One of the remarkable features of the play is the way it moves rapidly across Europe. The main scenes are set in the capital, Paris, in the court of the Countess of Roussillon in the southwest of France and in Florence, further to the south-east, where the hero, the Countess's son Bertram, goes to fight. These European locations may be seen to echo the capital, London, the seat of the Countess of Pembroke at Wilton House in the south-west of England, with foreign countries farther south-east. On top of this we can see the superimposition of further geographical parallels. The popular French King Henri IV had been in deep mourning when his favourite mistress had died in childbirth, and this led him in 1600 to look to Florence to marry the daughter of the Grand Duke of Tuscany, as the way to remedy the hole in the Bourbon succession.

The opening lines of *All's Well That Ends Well* are concerned with loss. Bertram is talking with his mother, the Countess of Roussillon, about his desire to go back to the French court.

The opening lines of the play, when the Countess is saying farewell to her son leaving for the King's Court in Paris, however low key, set the theme of loss:

COUNTESS: In delivering my son from me, I bury a second
            husband.
BERTRAM: And I, in going, madam, weep o'er my father's death
            anew (1.1: 1–2).

Almost immediately we learn of two important things: two bereavements and another bereavement waiting to happen. The

King of France is deathly ill with a fistula, which in medical parlance is a pathological opening rather like a junction box when two systems (rectum and bladder) become breached into one with the result that two spaces become one. The Countess suggests that help for the French King may lie in the hands of a young woman, Helena, who is staying at her palace and who has also suffered the recent bereavement of her father, Gerard de Narbon, known as such a famous natural healer that "he was skilful enough to have liv'd still, if knowledge could be set up against mortality" (1.1: 28–29).

It is not long before Helena is at the French court but she has a difficult task to persuade the depressed King that he will risk being healed. Indeed his pessimism comes to the fore when asked directly, "Will you be cur'd / Of your infirmity?" and he replies succinctly, "No" (2.1: 67–68). When he is eventually persuaded to try Helena's healing powers, which come, as she says, directly from her dead father, his reluctance to allow her even to try is expressed in a powerful statement of his ambivalence:

KING: Thou this to hazard needs must intimate
Skill infinite or monstrous desperate.
Sweet practiser, thy physic I will try
That ministers thine own death if I die (2.1: 182–185).

Helena, therefore, is put in a position of having to risk all if she is to heal the king, and she extracts from him a promise that if she is able to heal him she may choose any husband she likes from among the young courtiers. Despite the King's pessimism and reluctance to believe in her success, she is indeed successful and chooses Bertram. Bertram is horrified and, despite apparently agreeing, he immediately enlists his friend Parolles in working out a plan to take their sword and drum to the wars in Florence, packing Helena back to his mother in Roussillon. Although taking immediate flight from France, Bertram did leave Helena a letter, the terms of which set down some of the actions in the subsequent plot of the play:

HELENA: (reads aloud) "When thou canst get the ring upon my
finger, which never shall come off, and show me a
child begotten of thy body that I am father to, then call
me husband; but in such a 'then' I write a 'never'."
(3.2: 56–59) . . .
"Till I have no wife I have nothing in France." (3.2: 74)

She determines to go off on a pilgrimage to Saint Jacques (James), but instead of going west to Santiago da Compostella, following the well known pilgrimage route of the time, she goes east to Florence, where she gets wind of her betrothed's fame as a soldier, together with news of his sexual interest in a local girl, Diana.

There are two further important elements in the plot. The first is that at the time when Bertram is expressing sexual interest in Diana, Parolles loses his drum and creates mayhem among the soldiers, eventually being tricked by his colleagues into thinking that he has been captured. Blindfolded and under pain of torture and death, he is manipulated into betraying his colleagues, notably Bertram. The second important element of the plot is that Helena has organized and carried out a bed trick so that, instead of sleeping with the "chaste goddess" Diana, Bertram sleeps with her, the "pilgrim" Helena. Instead of dying in a convent as described to Bertram and later the King, Helena both captures the ring and becomes pregnant.

The last Act sees all the characters in the French court. The King sees the ring. Bertram invents a series of lies, but all comes out into the open and Bertram begs forgiveness, promising to Helena: "If she, my liege, can make me know this clearly / I'll love her dearly, ever, ever dearly" (5.2: 309–310).

In the Romance tradition, therefore, we are left, despite the psychological unlikelihood of such a miraculous transformation, thinking that he has learned and will continue to learn from his and Parolles' experience to pin his future hopes on her.

This play is a most striking exemplification of the creative working through of grief, but it also best exemplifies Rothenberg's thesis concerning the dynamics of creativity. Ted Hughes, the former Poet Laureate, in his book *The Goddess of Complete Being* (pp. 117–132), also explains why this is such a key play in initiating the greatest works of Shakespeare's maturity. Hughes, moreover, draws our attention to the remarkable intertwining of Bertram and Parolles in plot and sub-plot and sees them both as self-referential confessions of Shakespeare's own guilt.

I am suggesting that Shakespeare's Janusian thinking allows one to become two and his homospatial thinking for two to become one. These two processes are happening all the time, and the knife-edge of creativity therefore has to do with the relationships between these two processes, one becoming two and two becoming one. They create their own intercourse with its potential creative outcome in a play centring on death, sexual intercourse and birth and new generation, allowing the phoenix to be created anew.

Freud's concentration on actual sexuality and Jung's researches into the roots of hermaphroditism in such alchemical texts as the *Rosarium* (1550) can, perhaps, find a recreative synthesis in which both elements contribute helpful explanatory hypotheses. It is interesting that in Holland's book *Psychoanalysis and Shakespeare* (1979), the most comprehensive psychoanalytic study of *All's Well That Ends Well* at the time of its writing was an essay by Barbara Hannah (pp. 152–154), a close associate of Jung.

The phoenix arises from the alchemical fire, which is held in a creative container, into which La Feu (the steward of the Countess of Roussillon) helps to put Parolles and Bertram together. Through their manic mechanisms, which have to do with their man-ic part, getting caught up in identification with each other, two become one. In the fall-out of the alchemical fire, a different pairing emerges, that of Bertram and Helena.

If Parolles and Bertram begin in separation, go through humiliation together, and finally reach a creative separation, we can equally well look at the symmetry between Bertram and Helena. These two characters have both just lost their fathers, and are representative of two aspects or modes of reaction to mourning, the depressive internalization and the manic flight. Helena has taken to herself her father's most potent remedy and she sees herself as equipped in double strength, armed with a combination of masculine drive and potency with the most receptive sensitivity of her feminine, feeling side.

Just as we said earlier that it is very difficult to stay with the depressive anchor of the manic defence, so we do not easily see the anticipation pattern that is denied in mania. Bertram realized that he was trapped by his betrothal, surely because through sex he would be identifying, as a new married count, with his father, who has just died. The French king, when first greeting Bertram, makes the link clear:

KING: Youth, thou bear'st thy father's face;
          Frank nature, rather curious than in haste,

> Hath well compos'd thee. Thy father's moral parts
> Mayst thou inherit too! (1.2: 19–22)

Helena, therefore, has identified with her father by internalizing him so that she can be creative; Bertram, on the other hand, has identified with his father in such a way that he cannot cope with the situation of becoming an actual husband. He may have been able to tolerate the idea of being a metaphorical husband in relation to his mother, as the opening lines of the play showed, but to be married and to use his "thing" in marriage was too much for him. He felt "Till I have no wife, I have nothing in France" (3.2: 72) and therefore took refuge in flight. Our reading of the play would suggest that he takes flight in another direction, into a homosexual fusion with Parolles. It is striking that after the scene where Helena has been given to Bertram, the first time that we see Bertram and Parolles together Parolles addresses him as "sweetheart", not once but twice in as many lines:

BERTRAM: Undone, and forfeited to cares for ever!
PAROLLES: What's the matter, sweetheart?
BERTRAM: Although before the solemn priest I have sworn, I will
            not bed her.
PAROLLES: What, what, sweetheart? (2.3: 264–267)

Bertram's conscious object choice at this point in the play is for Fontibell, "a common gamester to the camp". On the Elizabethan stage, when played by a boy actor, she might well have looked like a male prostitute in drag. In fact she says her name is Diana, a representation of the chaste goddess Artemis.

A ring is a very frequent motif in Shakespeare (in *Two Gentlemen of Verona*, *The Merchant of Venice*, *Twelfth Night*, *Cymbeline*, for example). At one level it has to do with the potentiality of naught. Naught represents nothing, a creative empty space or a place where there is no "thing". The ring also represents the circular structure of the play as Helena at the end plays the physician to the "sick" Bertram. Parolles through the play has been associated, at least in Bertram's mind, with the drum, another circular object that contains a large quantity of empty air, but, as Parolles loses his drum, so Bertram turns his attention to Fontibell/Diana and her ring. He appears, therefore, to be switching his gender preferences and yet still wants to assert his independence through identification with Diana. She says "Mine honour's such a ring". She is identifying her honour, which is valuable, with the no-penis, the no-thing that is the ring. Just as she has a ring to give him if and when she chooses, so he has a ring to give her.

The ring represents the womb in this secret night substitution, in which in the act of intercourse two become one so that they can become three, or even, sometimes, four, if twins are the result. This was Shakespeare's own experience and it was also the case in the source that Shakespeare used for this play, where the "Helena" character became pregnant with twins. It is understandable, however, that Shakespeare should, in this play which ends with harmony and reconciliation, wish to change the twins into a single baby, as his own grief at the loss of one of his twins, his only son Hamnet, must have had powerful associations for him, even after five or six years. The play represents a coming to terms with grief and loss. Shakespeare's alteration of the source suggests that he was perhaps consciously aware that this process was not yet complete for him.

In this play we begin Act 5 with another minus one, namely Helena's supposed death, so that Diana can say of Bertram at the very end of the play:

DIANA: He knows himself my bed he hath defil'd;
           And at that time he got his wife with child.
           Dead though she be, she feels her young one kick.
           So there's my riddle: one that's dead is quick,
           And now behold the meaning (5.3: 294–298).

This brings us to the structure of Act 5, so often used by Shakespeare for final acts where the whole group meet together and, in the Romances at least, find themselves more than the sum of their parts, an experience that we can recognize when an analytic group is really working at full steam.

It is striking at the end of the play that so much of what came at the beginning is echoed. The King gives Helena to Bertram again. At the beginning Bertram deceived the King by giving only a half reply:

KING: Take her by the hand,
           And tell her she is thine; . . .
BERTRAM: I take her by the hand (2.3: 173–175)

At the end, however, Bertram, instead of giving a deceptive half reply, gives a double one:

HELENA: Will you be mine now you are doubly won?
BERTRAM: If she, my liege, can make me know this clearly, I'll
            love her dearly, ever, ever dearly (5.3: 308–311).

These last lines, which can be so difficult for modern audiences to take, need to be delivered with conviction and received quite literally, conveying Shakespeare's most powerful allegory of the now largely lost sixteenth-century belief in the neo-Platonic power of redeeming love. In this way the conversion of Bertram links up with a much earlier conversion, also psychologically improbable, of the wicked Proteus in *Two Gentlemen of Verona*.

All's Well That Ends Well, then, turns out in the end to be a play about the manic defence not being over-punished. At first, Parolles did appear to be over-punished for his empty parole-words, but at the end of the play La Feu looks after him and takes him back to Roussillon. Bertram, however, despite the manic flight both from the King in Paris to foreign wars and from the heterosexuality of marriage with Helena to a relationship with Parolles, has survived the war with bravery and honour and survived the potentially death-giving heterosexual intercourse.

In bringing this paper to a conclusion, I want just to consider very briefly the issues of unknown loss and double loss, because they have been my companions throughout the writing of this paper and they have helped to make being creative so difficult. A double loss is very difficult to mourn. Lady Bracknell's well-known lines, "To lose one parent, Mr Worthing, may be regarded as a misfortune; to lose both looks like carelessness" (Wilde, *The Importance of Being Earnest*, 1895, 1.1: p. 234), point to those emotions of guilt and shame that may accompany double loss; a double narcissistic blow, a double reason for the mechanisms of denial, and a double trajectory both outwards and inwards, railing in anger against others, against the world, against God or against the self in whole or part. But a double loss may also allow the possibility for double replacement.

My second companion, a missing friend, poses other difficulties along the same spectrum. It rushes back to the past, to the present and forward to the future in an unremitting, unresolved confusion.

I realize that the approach I have followed needs to be linked with the more obvious approach of bereavement and loss studies, both for individuals and for groups of different sizes. George Pollock of Chicago is a good guide in a review of this area of study in his article "The mourning process and creative organisational change". The earliest contribution he refers to is Van Gennep's classic anthropological monograph *The Rites of Passage* (1908, p. 22), where each rite of passage at every stage of the life cycle, examined in terms of order and content, consists of three major phases: separation, transition, and incorporation. Pollock contends, in psychoanalytic and clinical studies, that the mourning process is this adaptational transitional process and that the rites of transition are the group participation experiences allowing a social adaptation and thus a creative response to change. Just as the separation process is a "death", so each death is the birth of a new stage in each individual's development in some metaphorical form. Peter Marris, in his book *Loss and Change,* connects his studies of the experience of widows' groups undergoing social change by stressing loss factors as always involving the bereavement process. Watzlawick, Weaklend and Fisch, in their book *Change* (1974), has explored problem resolution in creative change as a function of the individual's or group's capacity to reframe their situation away from one that implies a future unchangeability. The ideas that are suggested by these studies may well refer to actual dying as well as to living through, and Parkes has shown us that old people are seven times as likely to die, literally from a broken heart, in the six months after their spouse's death.

The ideas of these writers take us into the heart of bereavement studies. Parkes, Pollock, Pincus and others have explored the factors making for pathological, as opposed to healthy, mourning. Support from the individual or group to face the actual reality of loss without recourse to denial is clearly crucial. But it is important to connect the reality of loss to the reframing of the potential impetus for optimism in the "empty space", despite its invitation to attract the manic responses of creativity. By accepting the sadness, and perhaps anger and guilt, about the minus one, the potential for plus one experiences is enhanced. In exploring collective responses to loss, we need to remember that the birth-rate rose in the Welsh mining community in Aberfan immediately after the avalanche that killed so many schoolchildren, and this included both those who had been and who had not been directly bereaved.

Martyrs always make for more converts, whether they be early Christians or the IRA, but in this connection I remember a very significant conversation I had with Max Hernandez, a friend and psychoanalyst in Peru, after he gave a moving talk about the situation of his own country at a conference in Delphi on "Tragedy". He was looking from a 400-year-old perspective at his country, where the massacre and destruction of the Incas in the sixteenth century was so complete—particularly since they had no written word to record their grief at what had befallen them. In consequence, the Spaniards and the indigenous population had never developed an integrated common ground to work on that original mourning process, which resulted, some while back, in the intractable problem posed by the Sendero Shining Path versus the government. Mexico, by contrast, had found common ground within a few years of Cortez's invasion, when the miraculous appearance of the Virgin and her subsequent shrine at Guadeloupe had brought together Spaniards with the local Mestizos in a common place of worship.

References

Bourne, S. (1992). *Psychological Aspects of Stillbirth and Neonatal Death: An Annotated Bibliography*. London: Tavistock.

Bourne, S., & Lewis, E. (1984). Pregnancy after stillbirth and neonatal death. *The Lancet, ii*: 31–33.

Earnshaw, A. (1995). *Time Will Tell*. Sydney: A and K Enterprises.

Freud, S. (1916). Some character types met with in psychoanalytic work. II, Those wrecked by success. *S. E., 14*: 304–333.

Goodwin, F. K., & Jamison, K. R. (1990). *Manic Depressive Illness*, Chapter 14. Oxford: Oxford University Press.

Hannah, B. (1955). *All's Well That Ends Well*: Studien zum analytische Psychologie C. G. Jung Festschrift zum 80 Geburtstag von C. G. Jung, 2B. Zurich: Rascher Verlag, II 344–363.

Hildebrand, H. P. (1988). The other side of the wall. A psychoanalytic study of creativity in later life. *International Review of Psycho-Analysis, 15*: 353–363.

Holland, N. (1979). *Psychoanalysis and Shakespeare*. New York: Octagon.

Hughes, T. (1992). *Shakespeare and the Goddess of Complete Being*. London: Faber.

Jamison, K. R. (1989). Mood disorders and seasonal patterns in British writers and artists. *Psychiatry, 52*: 125–134.

Jung, C. G. (1966). The psychology of the transference. In: *Collected Works of C. G. Jung, Vol. 16*. Princeton, NJ: Bollingen/Princeton University Press.

Marris, P. (1974). *Loss and Change*. London: Routledge & Kegan Paul.

Matte Blanco, I. (1975). *The Unconscious as Infinite Sets*. London: Duckworth.

Miller, A. (1958). *All My Sons*. In: *Collected Plays* (pp. 58–130). London: Cressset.

Parkes, C. M., & Williams, R. M. (1975). Psychosocial effects of disaster: birth rate in Aberfan. *British Medical Journal, 2*: 303–304.

Parkes, C. M., Benjamin, B., & Fitzgerald, R. G. (1969). Broken heart: a statistical study of mortality among widowers. *British Medical Journal, 1*(1): 740.

Pincus, L. (1974). *Death and the Family*. London: Faber & Faber.

Pollock, G. (1975). The mourning process and creative organisational change. American Psychoanalytical Association Post-presidential address, New York, December.

Rey, H. (1994). Universals of psychoanalysis in the treatment of psychotic and borderline states. *Free Associations* chapters 2, 13, 16.

Rosarium Philosophorum (1550). Frankfurt.

Rothenberg, A. (1979). *The Emerging Goddess*. Chicago, IL: University of Chicago Press.

Shakespeare, W. (1959). *Arden Shakespeare: All's Well That Ends Well*. London: Methuen.

Van Gennep, A. (1960). *The Rites of Passage*. London: Routledge & Kegan Paul.

Watzlawick, P., Weaklend, J., & Fisch, R. (1974). *Change*. New York: Norton.

Wilde, O. (1898). *The Importance of Being Earnest. Collected Plays, Volume I* (pp. 1–234). London:

CHAPTER THREE

The Caledonian tragedy*

Peter Hildebrand

During the course of Ronald Harwood's play and film, *The Dresser*, a leading character, the famous actor manager called 'Sir', inadvertently quotes *Macbeth* in his dressing room at the theatre. His dresser is horrified and implores him to take the appropriate action to exorcise the ill fortune that he fears will ensue. 'Sir' refuses, and after a brilliant performance of *King Lear* suddenly dies near the end of the play. We, the audience, are expected to assume that this is due in part to his action in quoting *Macbeth* and not then taking the appropriate steps to counteract the ill fortune that could follow.

The Dresser offers a good modern example of the theatrical superstitions that surround the tragedy of *Macbeth* by William Shakespeare. In a recent book entitled *The Curse of Macbeth*, Ronald Huggett (1981), gave some fifty pages of material describing how the play is regarded as unlucky or even accursed in the acting profession. Thus, the actors must never refer to the name of the play

---

*Previously published as Hildebrand, H. P. (1986). The Caledonian tragedy. *International Review of Psycho-Analysis*, 13: 39–48.

within a theatre. It is always called "The Scottish Play" or "Harry Lauder" or "That Play" or "The Unmentionable" or "The Caledonian Tragedy". *Macbeth* is associated with every possible form of ill fortune in the theatrical profession. When it is played, there is a history of theatres collapsing, actors falling ill, being injured in stage fights, running away, breaking down and actresses miscarrying. Famous actors and actresses playing the leading roles are reputed to have died soon after the play opened and the runs of many productions are associated with catastrophic experiences for members of the cast. Theatrical people, because of *Macbeth's* popularity, expected their companies to close when the play was put on, as it was usually regarded as a last resort by the management of a failing group to try and get an audience into the theatre. There have been actual deaths in stage duels and The Royal Shakespeare Theatre itself, at Stratford-on-Avon, burned down in the 1930s on the night following a performance of *Macbeth*.

As I have pointed out, it is considered extremely unlucky for an actor to quote *Macbeth* and the culprit must immediately go through a complex series of rituals in order to exorcise bad luck and counteract the effects of the curse. Huggett says that the traditional ritual is "To go out of the dressing room, turn round three times, to spit and knock on the door three times and beg humbly for re-admission" (1981, p. 62). A less powerful alternative is to quote the following line from *The Merchant of Venice*, a proverbially lucky play, "Fair thoughts and happy hours attend on you".

My purpose in this paper is to try and locate and explain these theatrical superstitions within a psychoanalytic framework. I shall draw on psychoanalytic theory, and also some structuralist ideas, in order to give a reading to the play that will clarify the reasons for the superstitions attached to it by the theatrical profession.

Macbeth, of course, is in many ways the most accessible and popular of Shakespeare's major tragedies—the story line is clear, the play is short, it contains some of the most beautiful poetry in the English language.

What is the play about? The eminent British director, Sir Peter Hall (1982), says

> *Macbeth* is the most thorough-going study of evil that I know in dramatic literature. Evil in every sense: cosmic sickness, personal

sickness, personal neurosis, the consequence of sin, the repentance of sin, blood leading to more blood, and that in a way leading inevitably to regeneration. Disease of crime or evil induces death, which induces life: *Macbeth* presents this cycle of living and in that sense I find it the most metaphysical of Shakespeare's plays-an unblinking look at the nature of evil in the person and in the state and in the cosmos. [p. 16]

But in my view, critics and directions have overlooked another major theme in *Macbeth*—that it resonates with a tremendously powerful but deeply hidden theme: incest, and, more specifically, mother–son incest.

It has always been my personal view—although my reading is not extensive, I have not seen it suggested elsewhere—that Macbeth should be played by a man in his early thirties and that Lady Macbeth should be played as a woman ten to fifteen years older than her husband, as a woman nearing the menopause.[1] In this interpretation, Macbeth is an intellectual, highly imaginative soldier who has symbolically married his mother. From the beginning of the play we are faced implicitly with the theme of incest. Recent studies of incest suggest that mother–son incest is the least well known, yet most frowned-on type of incest.

There are few psychoanalysts who have written about the play, so there is little in the literature that I can call upon directly in support of my hypothesis. Freud (1916d) wrote a paper on "Some character types met with in psychoanalytic work", in which he discussed Lady Macbeth in terms of the catastrophic failure of an ambitious personality. Freud felt that the action of the play was based on the contrast between the curse of unfruitfulness and the blessings of continuous generation, and explained Lady Macbeth's breakdown and death as a reaction to her being childless. However, beyond an approving nod towards Ludwig Jekels's (1917) theory that Macbeth and Lady Macbeth represent split-off aspects of the same person, he confessed himself unable to penetrate what he called the triple layer of obscurity in the play.

As in recent years psychoanalysts have written at length about Oedipus, and now the *Oresteia*, it is interesting that while these plays and *Macbeth* all treat the topic of incest, *Macbeth* has drawn little attention, which is striking, given the accessibility of the play itself. The answer may be found in the work of Lacan (1977) and in particular his seminar "The agency of the letter in the unconscious", in which he puts forward his thesis that 'The unconscious is structured like a language' and that to understand unconscious communication we have to understand the process of signification, of metaphor and metonymy, and, therefore, of the primary process. Lacan says,

> The creative spark of the metaphor does not spring from the presentation of two images, that is, of two signifiers equally actualized. It flashes between two signifiers one of which has taken the place of the other in the signifying chain, the occulted signifier remaining present through its (metonymic) connexion with the rest of the chain. [*ibid.*, p. 157]

He goes on to suggest

> The double-triggered mechanism of metaphor is the very mechanism by which the symptom, in the analytic sense, is determined. Between the enigmatic signifier of the sexual trauma and the term that is substituted for it in an actual signifying chain there passes the spark that fixes in a symptom the signification inaccessible to the conscious subject in which that symptom may be resolved—a symptom being a metaphor in which flesh or function is taken as a signifying element.
>
> And the enigma that desire seems to pose for a "natural philosophy"—its frenzy mocking the abyss of the infinite, the secret collusion with which it envelops the pleasure of knowing and of dominating with *jouissance*, these amount to no other derangement of instinct that that of being caught in the rails—eternally stretching forth towards the *desire for something else*—of metonymy. Hence its "perverse" fixation at the very suspension-point of the signifying chain where the memory-screen is immobilized and the fascinating image of the fetish is petrified. [*ibid.*, pp. 166–167]

I think hypotheses of this type may go some way towards illuminating why the hidden meaning of *Macbeth* has been obscured, and I think that this particular approach to literary criticism can be shown to have value not only for the psychoanalyst but for all those involved in the study and understanding of plays and poetry. Let me quote here Lacan's brilliant "Seminar on *The Purloined Letter*" (1972), which opens *Écrits* in French and which most beautifully demonstrates how the letter (of course, also in French *l'être*, the being) constitutes and changes meaning for each of the actors in the drama depending on the place that he or she holds. A reading of Edgar Allen Poe's story *The Purloined Letter* will demonstrate this quite clearly, but what Lacan reveals is also that possession of the purloined letter imposes on its holder a position that is unconsciously feminine—an action that not only complements, but actually overcomes, their active masculine behaviour, thought, insight, theft, penetration, and forces them into an identification with the feminine, so that, as he says, the letter that is so long in arriving becomes a fetish, a symbol of the maternal phallus. As a result the force of the story, which has held its place in the canon for 150 years, is due, in fact, to the unconscious understanding of the reader as to what is being investigated and communicated.

This approach is congruent to the one I take. Let us add to it Jekels' notion of Macbeth and Lady Macbeth as signifying two aspects of the same character—the same desire, if you like, and try to get a bit closer to the play and its characters.

Hall (1982) says,

> The dramatization of the relationship between Lady Macbeth and Macbeth *makes* the story happen. There are political ramifications, but the extraordinary basic tension is that between a great warrior, a great physical leader, and his wife. Macbeth is capable of hand-to-hand fighting and has enormous charisma, so that success comes naturally, but he is not in any sense an extrovert. His mask is that of an extrovert, but his actual sense is introverted, with a deep imagination, and a sense of fantasy with a rapid feverish ability to proceed from consequence to consequence like someone in a dream or nightmare. His imagination, even when he is happy and at peace, is restless. He is very perceptive, he studies himself . . . Macbeth knows himself, his own imagination, but Lady Macbeth has a very limited imagination, and this is why some actresses find the part unsatisfactory: they try to make it more than it is. I think it is a great role because she is a woman with little fantasy, little imagination, who is thoroughly practical, and thoroughly pragmatic. She is also very, very sexy; that is one of her holds on him, as it is one of his holds on her. [pp. 17]

Macbeth is a very martial man who is actually sensitive, poetic, and, in the best sense, feminine. He is always seeking these aspects of himself. Lady Macbeth is trying to complete herself to gain power through her identification with the martial hero. Each complements the other, and I think this is the source of their extraordinary capacity to understand and be close to one another.

I assume, along with most modern commentators, that the Folio version, which is the only one that we have, is authentic, and that the play opens with the witches on the blasted heath: in an ideal production—inside my head—I would show the witches wearing masks that are, at least in part, replicas of Lady Macbeth's face. I see no reason why, in a play that is about fantasy, superstition, and, of course, projection, the witches might not be interpreted as projected aspects of Lady Macbeth that have been renounced in the character herself. The witches announce a theme of the most profound ambivalence, "Fair is foul and foul is fair, / hover through the fog and filthy air". A theme which resonates—as Knights (1933) has shown—throughout the play.

The first human words we hear are, "What bloody man is that?" Blood is mentioned over a hundred times in the play. Hall says, "The man who is least likely to be able to kill because of his powers of imagination is the one who then killing bathes himself in blood. He doesn't just kill, he kills with a kind of celebratory relish!" Maybe Shakespeare kept such a theme within bounds by choosing such a man as Macbeth, the best at it. Blood is called for, blood is death and blood is life and blood must have blood. It has been well documented and well noted: *Macbeth* is the "play of blood". Blood and ambivalence, then, at once both themes emerge; we are given a report of Macbeth's prowess, Duncan awards him the title of Thane of Cawdor, there is a second appearance of the witches, and then Macbeth and Banquo enter for the first time. Macbeth's first words are, "So foul and fair a day I have not seen". In my reading this should be understood to refer not only to his present situation with the witches, but also to his relationship to Lady Macbeth, and his profound ambivalence about the relationship because of what it secretly implies. The witches know that Macbeth has become Thane of Glamis of his father's death, they predict that he will become Cawdor on Cawdor's death, of which he is still ignorant, and King thereafter. But having offered him such an exciting prospect, Banquo is immediately given more enduring hope: your children shall be kings hereafter. This introduces the third underlying theme of the play. Blood is symbolic of aggression, but blood as in blue blood or the blood royal carries the symbol of legitimacy and succession.

By a tremendous dramatic irony, immediately after awarding the Thaneship of Cawdor to Macbeth, Duncan awards the succession to the throne to his oldest son, Malcolm Canmore, so that Macbeth can no longer lawfully aspire to the throne. The succession has been snatched away from him and he and Lady Macbeth *have no children*.

I turn at this point to what I consider the seminal study of *Macbeth* in modern Shakespearian literature: Knights's (1933) famous lecture, "How many children had Lady Macbeth?" The title is ironic, a joust at those like Bradley, who treated Shakespearian characters as if they were real people and dissected their characterology as if they were psychiatric patients. Knights's question, which we may see as central to modern Shakespearian criticism, was, "How shall we read Shakespeare?" His answer is, "A play of Shakespeare is a precise particular experience, a poem" (*ibid.*, p. 132). He also says that the only full statement in language of this structure is in the exact words of the poem as conceived: but what the critic can do is to aid "the return to the work of art with improved perceptions and intensified, because more conscious, enjoyment" (*ibid.*). The function of the good critic is to point to something contained, and implicit, in the work of art. For Knights, "A poem works by calling into play, directing and integrating certain interests" (*ibid.*). Thus, "Macbeth is a dramatic poem", a revolutionary suggestion. I agree with this; in my view, it is a poem about incest, about blood and about the conflict between the gaining of power and the capacity to preserve it and pass it on, i.e., to father children, particularly sons, who can in that way ensure our own immortality, rather than trying to secure the illusory power of the maternal phallus.

As Knights points out, evil is poetically linked in the scheme of *Macbeth* with two main themes, the reversal of values and unnatural disorder. If my hypothesis has validity, then Macbeth has supplanted his father and Cawdor, who, I assume, must stand for Lady Macbeth's first husband, in Lady Macbeth's bed. He has married her for sexual passion, for her femininity, and to gain entrée into the royal circle, and thus the possibility of becoming King. For her part, Lady Macbeth has taken him for his force, his potency, and the possibility of controlling through him the springs of power. The Thane of Cawdor can throw away his life.

> . . . Nothing in his life
> Became him like the leaving it. He died
> As one that had been studied in his death,
> To throw away the dearest thing he ow'd,
> As 'twere a careless trifle. (4.1)

He is whole in himself, and can pay the highest penalty for a gamble lost. The resonance for Macbeth and Lady Macbeth is that they cannot ever accept such a fate, but instead have to strive against it.

Were it possible, they would have children. Their children, because of Lady Macbeth's blood tie to the throne, would in an elective monarchy have every chance of inheriting the Crown, but they cannot have children, if my interpretation is correct, since Lady Macbeth is past child-bearing age, and their union—like the fetish—must be barren. Nevertheless, like many older women in our culture, as Gutmann (1977) has shown, Lady Macbeth has become more aggressive and yearns for power. It is more than possible that in the Elizabethan world, such a yearning would be seen as unnatural.

The plot unfolds. Duncan comes to Glamis. Knights says

> What is not so frequently observed is that the key words of this scene are "loved", "wrongly", "bed", "procreant", "cradle", "breed", and "haunt", all images of love and procreation. Against the natural order of such things, the Macbeths oppose the spirits that tend on mortal thoughts. [1933, p. 143]

LADY MACBETH: . . . Come, you spirits
        That tend on mortal thoughts, unsex me here,
        And fill me from the crown to the toe top-full
        Of direst cruelty. Make thick my blood,
        Stop up th'access and passage to remorse;
        That no compunctious visitings of nature
        Shake my fell purpose, nor keep peace between
        Th'ffect and it! Come to my woman's breasts,
        And take my milk for gall, you murd'ring
        ministers,

> Wherever in your sightless substances
> You wait on nature's mischief. Come, thick night,
> And pall thee in the dunnest smoke of hell,
> That my keen knife see not the wound it makes,
> Nor heaven peep through the blanket of the dark,
> To cry, "Hold, hold!" (1.5: 39–53)

With this tremendous speech, Lady Macbeth denies her essential femininity and sets up her challenge for power, as she says to Macbeth, who hesitates before the object of his desire when they plan the murder of Duncan: "Leave all the rest to me".

The first act of *Macbeth* is one of the most stupendous pieces of writing in the literature. Shakespeare's profound knowledge of the human psyche is never more evident than when he gives Macbeth the soliloquy beginning, "If it were done, when 'tis done, then 'twere well / It were done quickly" (1.7: 1–2), which ends after talking of the planned murder of Duncan,

> MACBETH: And pity, like a naked new-born babe,
> Striding the blast, or heaven's cherubin, hors'd
> Upon the sightless couriers of the air,
> Shall blow the horrid deed in every eye,
> That tears shall drown the wind. I have no spur
> To prick the sides of my intent, but only
> Vaulting ambition, which o'erleaps itself
> And falls on th'other. (1.7: 21–28)

This sudden access of love and charity and identification with the child (the mother he is not and cannot be) is at once challenged by Lady Macbeth, so that Macbeth has to reply "I dare do all that may become a man; / Who dares do more, is none" (1.7: 46–47). The dramatic irony, once again, in the interpretation that I give to this scene, is that while he can murder the King, while he can be a valiant man of arms, he cannot father a child. Lady Macbeth, indeed, in the same scene says in reply to Macbeth,

> LADY MACBETH: . . . I have given suck, and know
> How tender 'tis to love the babe that milks me:
> I would, while it was smiling in my face,
> Have pluck'd my nipple from his boneless gums,
> And dash'd the brains out, had I so sworn
> As you have done to this.

MACBETH: If we should fail?
LADY MACBETH: We fail,
                But screw your courage to the sticking-place,
                And we'll not fail. (1.7: 54–64)

Lady Macbeth thus equates power with sexual competence—something which neither she nor the play can sustain. I think in this speech she manages to work Macbeth up by using her fertility as the goad that drives him to proving his virility by murdering Duncan. Indeed, it is clear that the murder of Duncan, which is, of course, central to the first part of the play, is a murder of the father, and that this parricide is also therefore the consummation of the incestuous act. As I say, Macbeth must murder Duncan to seize power, *yet* the poet presages his eventual failure in terms of unconscious phantasy in the soliloquy that begins,

MACBETH: Is this a dagger which I see before me,
           The handle toward my hand? Come, let me clutch thee:
           I have thee not, and yet I see thee still . . .
           There's no such thing.
           It is the bloody business which informs
           Thus to mine eyes. Now o'er the one half-world
           Nature seems dead, and wicked dreams abuse
           The curtain'd sleep. (2.1: 33–51)

Indeed, Lady Macbeth's next entrance, with a speech that ends, ". . . Had he not resembled / My father as he slept, I had done't. . . . / My husband!" (2.2: 12–13), I think reinforces the argument that I am putting forward here.

There follows the marvellous scene in which Macbeth conveys how his inner world has been changed by the act, and Lady Macbeth, who, surely at this point in the play could not be considered an imaginative woman, replies, "These deeds must not be thought / After these ways. So, it will make us mad" (2.2: 32–33).

Then, after the porter scene and various ominous presagings, Macduff returns to announce the murder, "Oh horror, horror, horror . . .", and Macbeth tells Malcolm and Donalbain, "The spring, the head, the fountain of your blood / Is stopped; the very source of it is stopped" (2.3: 98–99).

Macduff immediately reinforces the effect as we will see again with Banquo and others, "Your royal father's murdered" (2.3: 100).

The horrifying deed has been done and Macbeth justifies his secondary murder of the grooms, who surely must also symbolize Duncan's sons. Indeed there is some confusion in the stage direction, as to whether it is the grooms or Malcolm and Donalbain who are actually overheard by Macbeth and Lady Macbeth as they consummate the murder. Macbeth says, an overlooked but central speech in the play in which he tells us of his ostensible horror of the deed,

MACBETH: Who can be wise, amazed, temp'rate and furious,
           Loyal and neutral, in a moment? No man.
           Th'expedition of my violent love
           Outrun the pauser, reason. Here lay Duncan,
           His silver skin laced with his golden blood;
           And his gashed stabs looked like a breach in nature
           For ruin's wasteful entrance; there, the murderers,
           Steeped in the colours of their trade, their daggers
           Unmannerly breeched with gore. Who could refrain,
           That had a heart to love, and in that heart
           Courage, to make 's love known? (2.3: 108–118)

At this point Lady Macbeth faints and is carried out, and here I think the opposition of the two themes is complete, and one of the major signatures of the play is well and truly in place. The Macbeths have killed the father (Duncan) and seized power, and Macbeth, at the same time, has told Lady Macbeth that he has committed the supreme crime, parricide, for love of her, and thus symbolically consummated the incestuous act.

The motive for her faint is a point of considerable debate among scholars and directors. I quote Hall again:

> She might faint because she sees the consequence of the crime on Macbeth, the new ability with which he tells the lie, that is one possibility, or she may see all that is unleashed in the dramatic action, all those "Spirits that tend on mortal thoughts" . . . She sees them now: there they are, right in the head of her husband, or it may be that she actually faints under the general pressure of events, but that is rather a boring choice for an actress to make. [Hall, 1982, p. 21]

He continues,

This is one of the acts of bringing a play alive. There are often key moments which you can rationalise and say they must be that way or that way, but there is no absolute in these matters.

One of the basic strengths in Shakespearian drama is that the audience is shown what a character is actually motivated by and they then see him wearing a mask. This play is full of masks. [*ibid.*]

I think Macbeth penetrates the mask of the good hostess and conveys consciously or unconsciously to his wife, a most profound and profoundly disturbing message to her about their relationship, which we, the audience, have to understand, and which we can identify with in our own way: that that he has overcome the *horror* of incest.

Conrad Stein has written a most interesting book entitled *L'enfant imaginaire*, published in part in English under the title "Being alone with one's mother: the horror of incest" (Stein, 1984). In the book he suggests that all men have, at the same time, an incestuous wish and a horror of incest. All men, he says, nurture such wishes, and the horror of incest compels them to look everywhere for the stays that will guarantee that their desire will never be fulfilled.

If one considers that a great many calculate their chances for impunity with plans for transgressing every commandment except that which prohibits incest, one may indeed have the impression that incest is not a crime like others; that, not being the object of a temptation (for temptation is a conscious phenomenon), it has rather the permanence of a forever-hidden impulse and that the horror it evokes weighs a great deal more heavily than its prohibition. [*ibid.*, p. 273]

Perhaps this is why the witches have to be portrayed as supernatural temptresses. "The incestuous desire appears to be strictly connected to the horror of incest."[2]

It may well be that Banquo and Macbeth symbolize both sides of this feeling—Banquo is tempted towards murder, but has not the force or imagination to overcome his horror, Macbeth lays aside the mask and carries out the deed.

Macbeth succeeds to the throne, and the headlong pace of the play slows. He realizes that the witches' prophecy has come true,

"To be thus is nothing, but to be safely thus", and laments the fact that he may have acted,

MACBETH: To make them kings, the seed of Banquo kings!
            Rather than so, come, fate, into the list,
            And champion me to th'utterance! (3.1: 71–73)

One of the admirable things about *Macbeth* for an audience is that he accepts the consequence of his actions and he is going to go on fighting until he goes down into the darkness in the end. He already has, and we already have, an intimation that he has got things wrong, and that what he has done, with such courage, and such pain, will not have the results that he anticipates. Banquo and Fleance must die, yet again, Macbeth knows that his assault on their legitimacy will be as unnatural as his first unnatural mother.

Macbeth says,

> Come, seeling night,
> Scarf up the tender eye of pitiful day,
> And, with they bloody and invisible hand,
> Cancel and tear to pieces that great bond
> Which keep me pale. (3.2: 46–51)

The bond is love, friendship, security—bond is a most highly charged word: Banquo, who has kept to his bond, is killed, and perhaps it is no surprise that his ghost—the ghost of a desire that has been lived out—returns to haunt Macbeth. His answer is to seek out the witches again, for knowledge is power, to try to know his fate. He has a marvellous entry saying, "How now, you secret, black, and midnight hags, / What is't you do?" To which they reply, "A deed without a name" (4.1: 63–65).

It is perhaps worthwhile to say a few words about the witches here. They have always lent themselves to any amount of theorizing and clearly they can be produced as anything from genuine evil spirits to harmless old hags whose ravings Macbeth endows with power and phantasy. I feel that they should convey to the audience power and superstition—I see them both as projection of Lady Macbeth's phallic sexuality and also as the village abortionists, providers of simple medicines and coverers-up of things unsuitable for the sight of men, which they undoubtedly were in the seventeenth century. I think they express all the dark and hidden sexual and aggressive impulses that the men of that time feared and projected into the women who became the victims of the witch-hunts. Among their tasks were certainly abortions and the disposal of stillbirths, unwanted children, and the monsters one would expect from too close interbreeding, "The deed without a name".

The witches once again give Macbeth truthful but camouflaged prophecies, and confirm through the apparitions that whatever Macbeth may do, Banquo's descendants will inherit the Throne. Furious, Macbeth dismisses them and the scene changes for the working out of the tale.

Banquo is dead and Fleance fled, and it seems that the action of the play must slow down. Yet, what follows is fascinating in terms of a development of the theme of the contrast between the futility and sterility of the incestuous bond and the possibility of regeneration. I think that one way of looking at the complex thematic cross-currents that now emerge is in terms of the conduct of Macduff, since, after all, there are no absolute heroes and villains in the play. To our surprise, Macduff flees to England, leaving his wife and children at Macbeth's mercy. It is a passive act in the face of tyranny and Macbeth promptly has them murdered, breaking the usual conventions of Jacobean times, that whatever the political situation, dependants of your opponents would not be harmed. One might well pose the question whether Macduff, whom we later understand "is not of woman born" and is also therefore in conflict with ordinary development, unconsciously needs and uses Macbeth to murder them for him. Whatever the reason, using Knights' criterion there is little further we can say about it—poetically, the attack on the family and normal generation that runs through the play is most strongly reinforced.

"What, all my pretty chickens and their dam" cries Macduff, when Ross tells him of the murder—"He has no children".

For Knights, the whole discussion in the scene which follows between Malcolm and Macduff also has an emblematic quality—it conveys the contrast between the state of Scotland and the evils into which it has fallen and the opposite virtues that legitimate kings such as Edward, and Malcolm himself, personify, i.e., "Justice, Vanity, Temperance, Stableness".

So we come to the last act with its leaven of sublime poetry. I agree with Knights when he says, in contrast to an older school of critics,

It is no use saying that we are quietened, purged or exalted at the end of *Macbeth* or of any other tragedy . . . It is no use discussing the effect in abstract terms at all; we can only discuss it in terms of the poet's concrete realisation of certain attitudes and emotions. [Knights, 1933, p. 151]

For example, Lady Macbeth has run mad with guilt. The doctor says to the nurse

> You see her eyes are open
> NURSE: Aye, but their sense are shut.

But what she says makes very good unconscious meanings,

> LADY MACBETH: To bed, to bed: there's knocking at the gate. Come, come, come, come, give me your hand. What's done cannot be undone. To bed, to bed, to bed. (5.1: 63–65)

Hall says,

I've tried this scene many different ways. It still eludes me. I think it contains her whole life, her whole experience, not just the fragments of the murder; it has the perception of dreams. I honestly don't know what is the progression of this scene. It is not purgation. It may be that as Lady Macbeth leaves the stage, she has, for this instant of time, purged enough of her torment to have sleep. But I prefer to think that this is a segment of the journey towards death. As she says, "Give me your hand", and "to bed, to bed, to bed, to bed" the sexual bond, the life-giving bond, has been broken and there is a great desire to reinstate it—which we know will not happen. There are many new recognitions and great imaginative reach. I could make a case for the sleep-walking being a liberation of her imagination, so that she is almost like the early Macbeth when he roams imaginatively over the consequences of every action. She always has sensibility, but she had deliberately controlled it; now the blinkers are off. She is terribly clear-sighted.

The scene is pointless if it is the incoherent fragments of dream. It all has specific meaning, and a specific progress and development. And that's what is heart-breaking, perhaps; because I think the final effect on the audience must be to break their hearts. The doctor and the waiting woman tell us how to look at the scene—that's what they're there for, like different shots in a film—and finally they're struck dumb. [Hall, 1983, pp. 8]

My own interpretation would follow similar lines to that of Freud (1916d):

It would be a perfect example of poetic justice in the manner of the talion if the childlessness of Macbeth and the barreness of his Lady were the punishment for their crimes against the sanctity of generation . . . [p. 321]

So he points out

In Holinshed *ten years* pass between the murder of Duncan . . . and his further misdeeds . . . It is not expressly stated that it was his childlessness which urged him to these courses, but enough time and room is given for that plausible motive. [*ibid.*, p. 322]

But Freud is baffled by the fact that ostensibly in the play the course of its action covers *one week*! He says,

There is no time for a long-drawn-out disappointment of their hopes of offspring to break the woman down and drive the man to defiant rage; and the contradiction remains that though so many subtle interrelations in the plot, and between it and its occasion, point to a common origin of them in the theme of childlessness, nevertheless the economy of time in the tragedy expressly precludes a development of character from any motives but those inherent in the action itself. [*ibid.*]

If Freud is right, what we are presented with is a dramatic interpretation of Lady Macbeth's final failure of ambition and later-life aggression—a final breakdown of the intense mental effort she has had to produce to carry through her attempt to overcome the incestuous aim. In the end, it inevitably destroys her, her powers are not sufficient to overcome the headlong rush to disaster. She sees where the incestuous love, the sexual infatuation must lead and it destroys her.

Macbeth on the other hand, can and will fight. He has given up normal life span development,

MACBETH: I have liv'd long enough: my way of life
            Is fall'n into the sere, the yellow leaf;

And that which should accompany old age,
As honour, love, obedience, troops of friends
I must not look to have; but in their stead,
Curses, not loud, but deep, mouth-honour, breath,
Which the poor heart would fain deny, and dare not.
(5.3: 24–30)

He has also given up introspection, doubt, and uncertainty—alternatively cursing and pulling his armour on and off, he projects everything outside himself. He says to the doctor about Lady Macbeth,

MACBETH: Cure her of that:
Canst thou not minister to a mind diseas'd,
Pluck from the memory a rooted sorrow,
Raze out the written troubles of the brain,
And with some sweet oblivious antidote
Cleanse the fraught bosom of that perilous stuff
Which weighs upon the heart? (5.3: 41–47)

When the doctor replies, as might a modern therapist, "Therein the patient, / Must minister to herself", Macbeth replies, "Throw physic to the dogs; I'll none of it" (5.3: 48–49).

And then of course comes the sublime poetry of,

MACBETH: She should have died hereafter;
There would have been a time for such a word.
Tomorrow, and tomorrow, and tomorrow,
Creeps in this petty pace from day to day,
To the last syllable of recorded time;
And all our yesterdays have lighted fools
The way to dusty death. Out, out, brief candle!
Life's but a walking shadow; a poor player,
That struts and frets his hour upon the stage,
And then is heard no more: it is a tale
Told by an idiot, full of sound and fury,
Signifying nothing. (5.5: 16–27)

So well known to an audience that it must be one of the hardest speeches to bring off in the theatre. But the great soliloquy does not end the play. It is there for a dramatic reason—to underline the tendency of the last act, which is order emerging from disorder, and truth emerging from behind deceit. Once more my thesis is supported by a passage at the end of the play that again highlights the theme of legitimacy. Old Siward, the representative of the saintly Edward, is told that his son is dead.

Ross says,

> Your son, my Lord has paid a soldier's debt
> He only lived but till he was a man
> Like a man he died. (5.11: 4–8)

Siward replies,

> Had he his hurts before?
> . . .
> Why then, God's soldier be he!
> Had I as many sons as I have hairs
> I would not wish them to a fairer death;
> And so, his knell is knolled. (5.11: 12–16)

Then when Malcolm wishes to mourn young Siward, he dissuades him,

SIWARD: They say he parted well, and paid his score,
           And so God be with him! (5.11: 18–19)

Note the echoes of the death of the Thane of Cawdor.

The play ends with Malcolm's coronation and the promotion of the Thanes to earldom—the band of brothers is restored, Macbeth is slain, evil has been painfully overcome by active means, and order once more reigns.

I have suggested that there is a further theme behind the evil in *Macbeth*. I feel that a psychoanalytic reading of the play reveals more than the splitting and ambition which Freud perceived, it reveals a symbolic incest that, even though sterile, is passionate for power, actual power, sexual power, and political power. Stein (1984) says

> The horror of incest amounts to the fear of death. Its content is noth-ing—the nothingness of death connoted by an abstraction . . . The expectation of punishment inflicted by a jealous father or in the transference, the expectation of condemnation by the psychoanalyst

is superimposed on this horror and substituted for it as a representation capable of assuming the form of an image conforming to the
logic of a dramatic configuration. [*ibid.*, p. 19]]

I would add, like "The poor player who struts and frets his hour
upon the stage".

My final piece of evidence comes from anthropology. Claude
Lévi-Strauss (1969) has convincingly shown that human societies
structure their relationships to avoid incestuous relationships and
that exogamy, the marrying-out of children, both preserves the gene
pool and offers both economic and psychological security. Incest is,
therefore, almost universally feared, hated, and persecuted, and in
nearly all societies it is considered *unlucky*.

My conclusion, then, is that there is indeed a hidden evil
symbolically represented in *Macbeth*—the evil that is triggered by
the witches is the consummation of the incestuous relationship with
the maternal imago. The horror of incest is not that of parricide—
the father can be internalized after his murder by the band of brothers—it is the achievement of the conquest of and by the maternal
imago. We know that such sexuality, power without productivity,
may be a glittering prize, but is ultimately sterile. Both Jocasta and
Lady Macbeth play for the highest stakes wilfully, blindly but
unimaginatively, not knowing because not wanting to know what
they are doing. The tragedy, in one sense, is that Macbeth has the
power, imagination, and sensitivity to know what he is about, and
still he dares the impossible and unspeakable. Perhaps his nearest
modern equivalent is Mr Kurtz in Conrad's *Heart of Darkness* (1899),
whose last words were, "The horror, the horror". As Hall says,

There is something about living with evil which has a very debili-
tating effect on everybody. None of us likes to think that humans
have quite the capacity for evil. To recognize this in a play and to
recognize it in ourselves is a chastening and compelling experience.
[Hall, 1982, p. 30]

Which brings me full circle. The theatre, more than any other
form of art, symbolizes our phantasies and gives them temporary
life—what could be more understandable than that murder and
incest, "The deed without a name" should continue to be an object
of superstition and terror to the actors who have had, however

briefly, to embody "The Caledonian Tragedy" from its creation to the present day.

Notes

1. Parenthetically, the importance of early experience can be shown in this idea—one of the earliest and best performances of the play which I have seen was in Chicago in the early 1940s and starred a statuesque and quite elderly Judith Anderson as Lady Macbeth, while Maurice Evans, who seemed much younger, played Macbeth.
2. John Padel, whose brilliant psychoanalytic study of the Sonnets has opened new horizons for us on to Shakespeare's work (Padel, 1981), informs me that the Herbert family, for whom Shakespeare worked and wrote the Sonnets, was greatly troubled by incestuous relationships particularly in the generation before Mr W. Herbert, and that Shakespeare would certainly have been aware of and closely in touch with these developments at about the time he was writing *Macbeth*.

References

Conrad, J. (1899). *The Heart of Darkness*. London: Penguin, 1983.

Freud, S. (1916d). Some character types met with in psychoanalytic work. *S.E.*, *14*: London: Hogarth.

Gutmann, D. (1977). The cross-cultural perspective: notes towards a comparative psychology of aging. In: J. E. Birren & W. Schaie (Eds.), *Handbook of the Psychology of Aging*. New York: Van Nostrand.

Hall, P. (1982). Interview with John Russell Brown. In: J. R. Brown (Ed.), *Focus on Macbeth* (pp. 8–35). London: Routledge & Kegan Paul.

Harwood, R. (1980). *The Dresser*. Oxford: Amber Lane Press.

Huggett, R. (1981). *The Curse of* Macbeth *and Other Theatrical Superstitions*. Oxford: Amber Lane Press.

Jekels, L. (1917). The riddle of Shakespeare's *Macbeth*. In: H. M. Ruitenbeek (Ed.), *Psychoanalysis and Literature* (pp. 97–112). New York: Dutton, 1964.

Knights, L. C. (1933). *How Many Children Had Lady Macbeth? An Essay on Theory and Practice of Shakespeare Criticism*. London: Heffer.

Lacan, J. (1977). *Écrits*. London: Tavistock.

Lacan, J. (1988). Seminar on *The Purloined Letter*, J. Mehlman (Trans.). In: J. P. Muller & W J. Richardson (Eds.), *The Purloined Poe, Lacan, Derrida and Psychoanalytic Reading* (pp. 28–54). Baltimore: Johns Hopkins University Press.

Lévi-Strauss, C. (1969). *The Elementary Structures of Kinship*. London: Eyre & Spottiswoode.

Padel, J. (1981). *New Poems by Shakespeare. Order and Meaning Restored to the Sonnets*. London: Herbert Press.

Shakespeare, W. (1987) *The Complete Oxford Shakespeare*, S. Wells & G. Taylor (Eds.). Oxford: Oxford University Press.

Stein, C. (1984). Being alone with one's mother: the horror of incest. *Psychoanalytical Inquiry*, 4: 269-290.

CHAPTER FOUR

Some considerations of shame, guilt, and forgiveness derived principally from *King Lear*

Michael Conran

"Sorrow would be a rarity most belov'd,
If all could so become it." [*King Lear*, 4.3: 20–26]

I

I shall declare an interest. Some years ago my youngest daughter—I have three—said to me: "I am studying *King Lear* at school, will you talk to me about it?" We sat down on a park bench and talked for nearly an hour. Subsequently she asked me to write something for her. This took me, with twenty-one pages of foolscap, to the end of Act 1! As I attempted to proceed further I found myself drawn into something from which I was unlikely ever to be free, or wish to be free.

It is necessary to enter a caveat. When a psychoanalyst, addressing a celebrated literary text, announces it is not his intention to analyse either the text or the author, we are at once put on our guard that he is about to do just that. Since neither text nor author enjoys the private and exclusive relationship of a patient, both are available, promiscuously, to anybody and everybody, the text especially so. If the latter rivets our attention and captures our imagination, it can be said that a role reversal takes place, one having a certain psychotic quality: we (singularly) become the "patient" of the text. We feel we are "possessed" by it and then omnipotently "possess" it. The relationship is pre-oedipal in the classical sense, forsaking all others. For the moment we are alone with it. We suppose we are drawn to it by its manifest content. *Ars est celare artem* holds hands with psychoanalysis assuring the relevance of a *latent* content. Projection into the text and reintrojection take place. The "patient" discovers things in the text that *manifestly* are not there. Worse, he may ignore or distort things that *manifestly* are there. But even worse still he dares to infringe upon our private, exclusive possession. And, would you believe it, he doesn't know what he does and cares even less.

But there is more to it than that. Shakespeare has enriched us and our understanding of mankind in a way suggestive to us of his own working through. The *tout ensemble* is presented as something awesome in its majesty, so as to enhance our respect for and grati-tude to the man and his play, that he has given us so much. If I am now bold enough to seek to share my enrichment with others I may bring to some a new interest in the play. But if a colleague has had a close relationship with the play then beware! I shall have trodden on some corns. At best I shall be challenged—"what about this speech?", "what about that line?"; at worst—"Disgraceful! Reduc-tionist! Psychoanalysing Shakespeare!" and so forth.

Quite extraordinarily, both Shakespeare and the text survive, no matter what we do or say.

Moreover, we shall always remember that the characters in the play, as in any work of fiction, are not real people, however believ-able we find them. They are vehicles for the poet's psychological insights of mankind, at times, as we shall see, portrayals of the inner world of one person within two or more separate characters in the play. Such is the genius of the poet we are seduced into feel-ing about them, speaking and writing about them as if they were real people.

Charles Lamb (1912) was probably right to assert the Lear of Shakespeare cannot be acted. As he says, "When we read it *we are Lear . . .*" (my italics), which is to say that as we read we pause at our discretion to reflect upon ourselves, what Shakespeare is inviting us to ask of ourselves, to look at in ourselves with, if we dare, a seeing eye. Lamb had reason to know about madness, rage, and death. His sister murdered their mother with a kitchen knife and he devoted his life to her care.

It is necessary to say a word about the literature. In 1980 a two-volume annotated bibliography of criticism of Lear was published in the USA (Champion, 1980). It carries more than 2500 entries: more, it is said, than has been written about all the rest of the plays put together. Since then the pace has shown no sign of slackening. And this includes psychoanalytical writing. If each and every one of us is Lear, as Lamb says, why should we be surprised? So, if I say I shall give scant attention to the literature, my arrogance may be lost in my readers' relief. In dealing in madness it is necessary to resist the temptation to be over-inclusive.

Here then are two old men—Lear and Gloucester—set, as old men are, in the way of their death. Such are their fears of what lies ahead, they seek to engage their children, and others, in various processes of denial, seeking the status of an adult together with the security and ease of a child. In the course of this we become closely and painfully acquainted with their inner worlds; and the terrible price they pay, choosing between two forms of castration—blindness in one, madness in the other. Die they must and will, but such is the damage to their internal objects, we see this re-enacted, acted out, in defiance of guilt, so littering their way with pitfalls of their own making and pain sometimes scarcely bearable to witness.

There are two blood-curdling moments in the play which cause the audience to gasp with horror. The first comes in Act 1 when Lear, frustrated, curses his daughter Goneril:

LEAR: Hear, Nature, hear! dear Goddess, hear!
Suspend thy purpose, if thou didst intend
To make this creature fruitful!
Into her womb convey sterility!
Dry up in her the organs of increase,
And from her derogate body never spring
A babe to honour her! If she must teem,
Create her child of spleen, that it may live
And be a thwart disnatur'd torment to her!
Let it stamp wrinkles in her brow of youth,

With cadent tears fret channels in her cheeks,
Turn all her mother's pains and benefits
To laughter and contempt: that she may feel
How sharper than a serpent's tooth it is
To have a thankless child! Away, away! (1.4: 254–269)

The other occurs later when, at the behest of Lear's daughters
Goneril and Regan, and as a consequence of Edmund's conspiracy,
Gloucester's eyes are gouged out on stage. It must be evident that
there is no way back either from curse or deed. The destruction is
as irreparable as it is irretrievable.

Noel Hess (1987) in a study of Lear and some anxieties of old
age derived from consultations with elderly patients in primary
care, described a fundamental anxiety of old age: the dread of being
abandoned to a state of utter helplessness. Hess, from these consultations, was able to add to Jaques's (1965) description of the unconscious phantasy of imminent immobilization and helplessness, in
which the self is subject to fragmentation while retaining the capacity to experience persecution and torment. Hess adds a terror of
being left alone, not just without a spouse or loved object, but without an organizing or containing part of the self, which is felt to be
lost in the catastrophes of old age: stroke, injury, illness, and demen-
tia. Hess draws upon this to expose the tyranny of Lear, the exac-
erbation of his narcissistic injury, his denial of vulnerability,
contemptuously equated with femininity:

LEAR: And let not women's weapons, water drops
         Stain my man's cheeks . . . [2.4: 275–276]

It will be apparent that we, psychoanalysts and others, have
moved far away from an acceptance of Lear and Gloucester as mere
unfortunate victims of filial ingratitude and evil.

Ella Freeman Sharpe (1946) sailed in, firing every analytic shot
at her disposal, the text and poet conjointly the target of her analysis, having carefully set out the rules by which she will proceed,
and seeing the play as the four-fold "howl" put into words. For her,
Lear's three daughters represent three different projected aspects of
one mother. Through Lear, Shakespeare is said to reveal his early
feelings about his own mother and, "more complicated, those experienced towards his father", as represented by the cruel Cornwall

who must die, the ignorant Albany who will live, and the King of France who is left alive without Cordelia. She suggests Shakespeare was incontinent at the age of 2½, before his brother's birth; that the knights are symbolized faeces; that "Goneril with a white beard" tells of a repressed knowledge of menstruation, bandage, and pubic hair—all this and more, much more, in an *analysis* which is at once riveting, convincing, and yet somehow ridiculous. Ridiculous, not because it is in any way lacking richness and scholarship, but because it invites ridicule from two directions: from that conviction which, in its finality, defies further argument; or just angry, uncomprehending rejection. Of one thing I am sure, whatever is made of her analysis, it is not going to go away. Critics will find the invitation to read it, so to ridicule it, irresistible. Once read, her analysis, as an example of criticism at its most delinquent, or eloquent, or both, will have a life in the unconscious, if nowhere else.

A psychoanalytic interpretation by Roberto Speziale-Bagliacca (1980) directed attention to the nature of the authoritarian, tyrannical personality of Lear, drawing on Rosenfeld's sadistic narcissism (Rosenfeld, 1965), Fairbairn's internal saboteur (Fairbairn, 1952), and the phenomena that result in the dictatorship of internal objects. To this must be added the work of Steiner (1982), where goodness, contained in the healthy parts of the self, colludes with and allows itself to be taken over by the bad, delinquent, narcissistic organization. From this, Likierman (1987) derived a differentiation of anger, between constructive and destructive anger. She considers rage to be destructive, psychotic anger, of which Lear is taken as an example. Rage is seen as a consequence of reality, however trivial, becoming a threat to an elaborate defence system, a system based upon self-deception.

Likierman focuses upon Lear's rage in the face of his daughter's insistence upon her resolute individuality. She might well have added:

LEAR: I will have such revenges on you both
         That all the world shall—I will do such things,
         What they are, yet I know not, but they shall be
         The terrors of the earth. (2.2: 453–456)

These are the impotent, raging threats of a child in the frustration of a tantrum, seeking to destroy a persecuting world. The tantrum of a child is sheer madness in an adult. In a king, or any ruler, it is a Hitlerian spectre—terrifying to the whole world.

Let us now heed the words of another woman, still living, speaking of her father: a ruthlessly ambitious man who became an unchallenged leader. To his small daughter he was an indulgent father.

> My childhood was a happy time, a paradise of sorts. My father was very demonstrative, holding me on his lap and cuddling me. . . . I was his favourite because I resembled his mother and he would say: "It's ridiculous, it's just funny how much you look like my mother!" This pleased him.

As she grew older his doting affection declined. He liked women to be passive, compliant, and his daughter had a mind of her own.

> When I was a child I was a pet and fun and relaxing, and that he liked. Later, when I started showing some signs of independence, he didn't like it at all. . . . Then I really fell out of favour with my father because I fell in love with the wrong man while I was still at school.

The woman is Svetlana Peters (Alliluyeva) speaking about her father, Josef Stalin (Lambert, 1990).

This takes us now to the opening scene of the play, wherein we give attention to the words of Coleridge (1818) and Charles Hanly's review (Hanly, 1986). In consideration of Lear's treatment of his daughters, Hanly reminds us of Coleridge's insistent attention to the degradation and humiliation of Edmund by his father, and how he (Coleridge) "has demanded of us that we seek an understanding of the evil of Edmund, *without forgiving* the evil he does . . ." (p. 212, my italics). The curtain rises. We are scarce settled in our seats when, within the space of a minute, we are tittering with ribald amusement. We have been engaged to identify with a witty old man, Gloucester, while he splits off and projects a *shameful* part of himself, *shamelessly*, into his helpless, illegitimate son Edmund, having remarked how Lear esteems his two sons-in-law equally. The boy, now a fine figure of a man, stands there trapped, as near to his father as he is ever allowed to come,

GLOUCESTER: He hath been out nine years, and away he shall again
        . . . (1.1: 31)
while his father rubs his son's nose in the primal scene:

> . . . there was good sport at his making, and the
> whoreson must be acknowledged. (1.1: 22–24)

Our *shameless* sniggering is barely spent as we are propelled
with electrifying rapidity into the public love auction, whereat Lear
shamelessly humiliates his two elder daughters, Goneril and Regan,
married but not yet dowered. Is it to be supposed this is the first
time these women have been exposed, *shamefully* for them, *shamelessly* by their father? If love is not to be deserved, it most certainly
cannot be purchased.

But as Kent will later tell us, "A sovereign shame so elbows him
. . ."

The shame of the man keeps him, with the help of projective
identification, from any relationship which threatens to penetrate
and shatter those illusions, like the collapse of a house of cards,
upon which he supposes his integrity—his sanity—depends.
Cordelia utters just such a threat and painfully penetrates his false,
fragile, mental skin with truth.

LEAR: [to Cordelia] So young and so untender?
CORDELIA: So young, my Lord, and true.
LEAR: [explodes in rage] Let it be so; thy truth then be thy
        dower. (1.1: 106–108)

So economical is the poet with words, so compressed is the richness
of meaning as to invite minute and detailed attention. Small
wonder then the psychoanalytic as well as the literary fascination
with this play.

II

It is at this point I wish to reflect upon this matter of shame, shame-
fulness, shamelessness, and their many close relatives: humiliation,
degradation, and embarrassment, to mention only three. This in
contrast with guilt, for which remorse is the only close relative that
comes to mind.

If shame is a Medusa-like creature to which Freud gave little attention, it has recently become a field rich in psychoanalytic exploration. However, my interest is less in shame by itself, rather in its relationship to mindlessness, guilt, and that *acceptance* implicit in forgiveness.

The matter is psychoanalytically complicated by two further differentiations: guilt bearable and unbearable; and a distinction drawn between depressive guilt and persecutory guilt.

Guntrip (1964), examining the concept of *guilt*, pointed out the differences between moral, judicial, and emotional guilt. He termed the latter, emotional guilt, "shame". He saw the problem facing the therapist as "inordinate shame", i.e., either shame when there is obviously no guilt in reality, or a total lack of shame when the guilt was apparent (Marteau, 1988). The inference I draw from this is that patients do not, whatever they say, bring guilt to analysis. Shame and the fear of shame may masquerade as guilt; but it seems to me the experience and containment of guilt is a very special matter.

Kinston (1987) has argued that the move from *mindlessness* to shame is a move counter in direction to the death instinct. It seems to me useful to think of a continuum of mindlessness through shame to guilt, perhaps not dissimilar, nor necessarily far removed from Klein's paranoid–schizoid and depressive positions; from invulnerability to vulnerability; from pre-ruth to concern (Winnicott, 1955).

Whereas there can be movement, backwards and forwards, a continuum presupposes two or more positions cannot be occupied concurrently.

Depressive guilt, which I shall call guilt, is that which is inseparable from sad feeling and a reflective state. This depends, in my view, upon internal good objects sufficiently *accepting* to be felt to be capable of *forgiveness*.

The capacity to forgive oneself presumes an apparatus—internalized forgiving parents—wherewith normal sad feelings and guilt can be experienced. Sad feelings can find comfort, guilt can find forgiveness.

In the absence of, or the inadequacy of such a good object or objects, forgiveness is not possible, and then the risk of the experience of guilt cannot be taken, since it cannot be borne. It may then be split off and projected *shamelessly* as *shame*. It will be projected even into the unforgiving object which then becomes the persecutor, i.e., the source of persecutory guilt, so-called. The lamentation of *mea culpa* is a blanket denial, like a smoke-screen. "I am guilty"— of everything and nothing—in avoidance of the pain of admitting the particular. Unconscious guilt, along with somatic manifestations, may be found to fall into this category, the abiding principle being the inadmissibility of pain into consciousness.

The child seeks parental forgiveness, but the adult is presumed to have such internal objects as enable him to forgive himself. That is why Yehudi Menuhin, addressing the Open University some years ago, said, "We cannot forgive the German people for the Nazi atrocities: they must forgive themselves." It also accounts for the palliative forgiveness of the Church of its adult "children", who seek forgiveness from others in order to make life bearable. It further explains the intense irritation we feel when, patronizingly, we are offered gratuitous forgiveness.

The internal objects are experienced as forgiving not only of the child, but of others too—above all, of each other. The capacity of parents to forgive each other will colour a child's view of the primal scene. And it will not be forgotten that we can only guess how many of us came into this world as the consequence of an act of forgiveness!

Guilt and shame are, as I have indicated, incompatible: one or the other, but not both together. It is as if shame bears a relationship to guilt as envy to jealousy—a two-person or a three-person phenomenon. Indeed, I would go so far as to say shame is the poison of guilt, since the experience of *shame is wholly antithetical to thought*, upon which guilt depends.

Shame, so it seems to me, operates superficially—I use the word in a mentally topographical sense. It operates at the interface of body and mind, which is why I put it in a continuum with guilt and mindlessness. Its physical component may be such as to threaten the integrity of the self. Yet it reminds the self of a body that feels, even to be threatened. Clifford Yorke (1989) has recently expressed this similarly, stating that shame is neither wholly internal nor wholly external to the self.

Reference needs to be made to shame cultures and guilt cultures, so-called (Rycroft, 1968; Thubron, 1987). Perelberg (1980) has shed further light on this in her examination of the distinction made by an Afro-Brazilian cult, "Umbanda", between the individual and the *persona* as distinct targets for the allocation of responsibility. This is beyond the scope of this paper, except to note that any army and, therefore, any nation-state committed to war, must assume the attributions of a shame culture, i.e., shame avoidance, if it is to fight at all.

The shame that I am considering in the context of *King Lear* is of a frightening order. It excites fight and flight responses. But we shall remember that shame comes by degree. To be embarrassed for example, is to feel alive, sometimes quite enjoyably. But when there is a threat to that which enables the self to distinguish body from mind, wherein the mental skin is breached, such that everything may get out and get in, then defences of the most drastic kind are invoked: flight by denial; fight by projective identification. The circularity or self-promoting nature of these processes secures a repetition of shaming, being shamed, or a retreat to mindless action in the preservation of the mental skin.

To "open up", as we say, to "own up" and to "admit", is to throw open a door, to permit a breach and let responsibility deeply into the self: in short, to admit guilt and to acknowledge, in the words of Gloucester's legitimate son:

EDGAR: . . . Men must endure
           Their going hence, even as their coming hither:
           Ripeness is all. . . . (5.2: 9–11)

In contradiction of:

LEAR: . . . tis our fast intent
           To shake all cares and business from our age . . .
           (1.1: 38–39)

which is not a responsible option.

Owning up, taking responsibility for one's thoughts and deeds, retrieving one's projections, admitting guilt and so, abandoning Lear's lament, "I am a man / More sinn'd against than sinning" (3.2: 59–60), depends then, in my submission, upon that *inner acceptance* we call forgiveness. Forgiveness, then, in adult life, can only truly come from within, from objects such as I have described, felt to be forgiving of the transgressing child. This does not exclude anger and the temporary withdrawal of love.

Coleridge is therefore correct to insist we cannot forgive the evil Edmund has done. Our task is to understand it, which is quite another matter. His treatment by his father and the denigration of his mother, and, above all, the manner of his exposure to the primal scene, robs him of objects with which he could forgive himself. He is then just as much "bound upon a wheel of fire" as Lear. For Lear, similarly, has in his own words and therefore in his own mind, done things that unarguably are the terrors of the earth.

In contrast to the blinded and so inwardly seeing Gloucester— seeing his way feelingly and so able to retrieve his projections— Lear dare not open himself. For Lear, to let in, to admit, as to let out, is to go mad.

LEAR: . . . Old fond eyes,
           Beweep this cause again, I'll pluck ye out,
           And cast you, with the waters that you loose,
           To temper clay . . . (1.4: 281–284)

As his defiance is further challenged and his defences threatened to breaking point:

           You think I'll weep;
           No, I'll not weep:
           I have full cause of weeping, but this heart
           Shall break into a hundred thousand flaws
           Or ere I'll weep. O Fool! I shall go mad. (2.2: 456–459)

The stage direction—"storm heard in the distance"—comes in the midst of that speech. The storm, which all his life he has sought to contain, is about to become containable no longer. It is the storm wherein his objects were irretrievably destroyed. Within the racket of the storm he may hide from a feeling, persecuting world. With the help of lightning he may split, as lightning splits, himself off from all feeling. Thunder will serve a dual purpose, bringing all to their knees, drowning out all cries; above all, quelling, rendering inaudible any inner feeling voice.

Hitherto his madness has been represented to us as conduct by which he deals, however inadequately, with his fear of madness.[1] But this is now past and all can see what can no longer be hidden. His madness, like a dog, will have its day.

III

It is necessary to give special consideration to the Fool.

The Fool appears before Lear's frustrating encounter and in the wake of Cordelia's banishment. Having banished her from his sight, Lear fidgets restlessly: "Where's my Fool, ho? . . ." He is answered: "He says, my Lord, your daughter is not well."

The Fool and Cordelia are clearly connected with each other. There is even a momentary confusion in our minds for whom he is calling.

He is told that since Cordelia went to France: ". . . the Fool hath much pined away."

LEAR: Go you, call hither my Fool. (

Some part of him, it seems, is missing. Projective identification leaves the self denuded, empty. Having projected his bad, shameful feeling into his daughter and banished her, her upon whom he depends and will seek to depend further, he is a man bereft, aimless. He cannot have her back, she who speaks truth. Except perhaps, in the guise of a boy, one held at a distance, a part of himself yet apart from himself, heard not heeded. Like the boy who saw the Emperor wore no clothes, the Fool may speak truths that can be heard—indulgently, patronizingly and with amusement—heard but not received. Truth, in the sense used by Shakespeare, is what we would now call psychic reality. In the last speech of the play, Edgar will entreat us all to "Speak what we feel, not what we ought to say" (5.1: 300).

An adult, non-psychotic part of Lear's personality can be tolerated, encapsulated, disguised; lovable and tender yet impotent to penetrate his fragile mental skin with his comic insights. Put simply, it seems the King has found a device, to wit the Fool, whereby he may tell himself home-truths which, though coming from within, can be tailored in such a way as not to interfere with the progression of his rage to madness and the avoidance of grief. In the Fool, according to my reading, Shakespeare anticipates Freud's (1940e) discovery of splitting of the ego.

The Fool tells Lear of a fellow who banished two of his daughters "and did the third a blessing against his will". We know he did not banish Goneril and Regan, only Cordelia. In this way, as has been pointed out, he banished the elder daughters permanently from his and their love; whereas he set Cordelia free to marry France, who loved her unconditionally (dowerless), and so spared her the venal Burgundy.

The Fool, then, is dependable, a steadfast crutch, a link to reality enabling Lear to carry on a self-deception of narcissistic self-sufficiency. He is proof against the eruption of incestuous feeling and the conflict that entails. He is, above all else, a repository for psychic pain.

FOOL: . . . they'll have me whipped for speaking true, thou'll
          have me whipped for lying, and sometimes I'm
          whipped for holding my peace. I had rather be any
          kind of thing than a fool, and yet I would not be thee
          . . . (1.4: 16)

The Fool disappears from the play in anticipation of the return of Cordelia, who has a particular function in helping Lear to die.

In the end, Lear makes a final surrender of this split off, little boy part of himself at the beginning of his last speech, with what is really an aside, referring to something which again invites a momentary confusion: "And my poor fool is hang'd! . . ." (5.3: 281). Cordelia and all the Fool has represented are about to become one with the object. (It is hardly to be wondered that it has been suggested both parts, the Fool and Cordelia, might have been acted by one and the same player.)

The parallel of this relationship of the Fool and Cordelia with Lear is to be found in the relationship between Edgar and his now blind father, Gloucester. Gloucester, too, has split off and projected unwanted guilt into Edmund, his paranoid fears of betrayal and parricide into Edgar who, if he is to survive, has to assume the guise of madness. In a mad, murderous world, feigning madness may be the only route to survival. Thus "poor Tom O'Bedlam" takes on in this relationship an equivalent part of the Fool, except that he becomes the repository of Gloucester's dissimulation and hypocrisy. The capacity to be a hypocrite denotes the existence of an ego sufficient such that it can be compromised. Gloucester therefore has no need to go mad, much though he would welcome the relief it brings. Advised by Cornwall to "come out o'th'storm", to leave the King to his madness, he turns a blind eye: he denies, what must be the castrating consequences of his projections.

Once blinded, the only sight available to Gloucester is insight, demonstrated in the following exchange with Lear:

LEAR: No eyes in your head, nor no money in your purse?
             Your eyes are in a heavy case, your purse in a light:
             yet you see how this world goes.
GLOUCESTER: I see it feelingly. (4.5: 41–44)

With the help of Mad Tom (Edgar) he will find a natural reunion with the object.

IV

In consideration of the death of Lear we return to Freud (1913f), to the essay "The theme of the three caskets", surely at the centre of any psychoanalytic thinking about the play. Freud charges Lear that he should accept Goneril and Regan's view of the proper meekness of the old and, in his words, that he should "renounce love, choose death, and make friends with the necessity of dying" (p. 301). Cordelia's silence, it is most convincingly argued, betokens death and that we must accept the inevitability of death. What, we may ask, are the conditions of such acceptance? Put in another way, how does a man die who has little capacity for self-acceptance, of self-forgiveness?

LEAR: A sovereign shame so elbows him: his own
             unkindness,
             That stripp'd her from his benediction, turn'd her
             To foreign casualties, gave her dear rights
             To his dog-hearted daughters, these things sting
             His mind so venomously that burning shame
             Detains him from Cordelia. (4.3: 43–48)

If Cordelia is death and he must die, what are we to make of his detention? Gloucester, blind but seeing clearly says:

GLOUCESTER: The King is mad: how stiff is my vile sense
             That I stand up, and have ingenious feeling
             Of my huge sorrows! Better I were distract:
             So should my thoughts be sever'd from my griefs,
             And woes by wrong imaginations lose
             The knowledge of themselves. (4.5: 274–279)

Muir (Shakespeare, 1972) explains that "Gloucester calls his senses vile because they still allow him to be fully conscious of his sorrows, and do not give him the relief of insanity". Blind, yet seeing inwardly, preferring madness, but he is able to suffer his pain in forgiveness of himself. Able to experience, bear and suffer his own pain in self-acceptance, he can take responsibility for his own mental life.

Shakespeare explains, demonstrating how Gloucester admits his guilt:

GLOUCESTER: O my follies! Then Edgar was abused.
Kind gods, forgive me that, and prosper him
(3.7: 90–91)

and

. . . Oh! Dear son Edgar,
The food of thy abused father's wrath;
Might I but live to see thee in my touch,
I'd say I had eyes again. (4.1: 23–26)

There is no more tender moment in the play as Gloucester owns up, acknowledges, and admits his guilt, unaware of the presence of his son. It is an admission as opposed to a *confession*, which would be in the nature of a projection of pain.

He continues:

GLOUCESTER: I have no way, and therefore want no eyes;
I stumbled when I saw . . . (4.1: 20–21)

Having no way to see he can, inwardly, see his way to death and, as we learn, to reconciliation with the wronged son Edgar.

GLOUCESTER: . . . Henceforth I'll bear
Affliction till it do cry out itself
"Enough, enough," and die. (4.6: 75–77)

The reciprocal of this is found in the object, now Edgar, in his reply to Albany's question:

ALBANY: How have you known the miseries of your father?
EDGAR: By nursing them, my lord. (5.3: 179–180)

As we shall see it is a task Cordelia has been called to and will be called to again when Lear pleads with her, attempting to confess some notion of his guilt, to retrieve some projections, as when he says to Cordelia:

LEAR: . . . weep not:
               If you have poison for me, I will drink it.
               I know you do not love me; for your sisters
               Have, as I do remember, done me wrong:
               You have some cause, they have not. (4.7: 71–74)

He seems to say "If you can find it in you to love me, which I do not deserve, you may forgive me and then I can own up to what I have done to you". But he cannot resist the temptation to divide her (Cordelia) from her sisters—"You are good, they are bad".

What father, in the face of his death, could not but yearn to see his children lovingly united? Not so Lear, still contriving to divide and rule. His guilt remains *inadmissible* to the end, as we shall see.

Freud (1920a) was nowhere so lastingly controversial as in his formulation of that drive implicit in our lives towards disconnection and death. I say disconnection because it represents more than a disconnection with external reality but with internal object relationships too. All relationships, internal as well as external, are finally abandoned in death. It is an anti-inflammatory impulse, in every sense, for which we have been able to find no better expression than "death instinct". It is as if we must, in the coupling of these two words, negate, and so give death to, a word—instinct—whose meaning is inseparable, in our minds, from life.

To court and to befriend one's own death is to yield by degree to a reciprocity, simply expressed as both possessing and being repossessed by the object. The anticipation of death promises relief and safety and the end of a struggle for which ageing renders the self increasingly unequal. It implies a return to infantile omnipotence and helplessness.

Kent speaks of the death of Lear:

KENT: Vex not the ghost: O! let him pass; he hates him
               That would upon the rack of this tough world
               Stretch him out longer. (5.3: 313–315)

This is echoed by Lamb (1912) in defiance of Nahum Tate's contrivance of a happy ending: ". . . as if . . . the flaying of his feelings alive, did not make a fair dismissal from the stage of life the only decorous thing for him" (p. 18).

I wish to turn away, for the moment, to what other poets and prose writers have contributed to this matter of reunion with the object.

Boris Pasternak (1958) contrives the death of Zhivago in a curious way. Zhivago struggles to leave the tram, the tram that carries him haltingly and inadequately (though enrailed) through the last moments of his life. Alongside the tram, on the pavement, a woman in a lilac dress hurries: now overtaken by the tram, now overtaking it, as it breaks down repeatedly. Apparently she, a Swiss national, has no relevance to the novel other than that she is known to us in those the last moments of Zhivago's life, as he struggles to be free of the tram only to fall dead in the street. What, we may ask, is the latent meaning of the poet's fiction?

Does not Ibsen have Solness, in *The Master Builder*, nearing sixty, "bound upon a wheel of fire"? Driven from an impossible impasse in his life towards death as his only solution, a young woman of twenty-three comes for him. In its manifest content her transference to him has no connection with his to her. But in its latent content she will neither deny him nor be denied by him. Acceptance and love will carry him, through her, to death.

In "Colloquia con la madre", Pirandello (1915) introduces us to a further dimension of man's relationship with his mother in the face of his death. Tired of life, he returns to Kaos to his childhood home near Agrigento, Sicily. In his imagination he discovers his mother, many years dead, and converses with her. Aware of his suffering she asks: "Am I not perhaps always alive for you?" To which he replies: "Oh! Yes, Mamma! You are alive indeed. . . . But that is not the point . . . The point is that I now am no longer alive for you and never shall be again. Because you cannot think of me . . ." His need is, in fantasy, to bring her to life, to think of him, so to accept him, if he is to find reunion in death.

There is then the man who set us free to think unthinkable things. Freud himself identified with Lear's peevishness in the face of his daughters' ingratitude. In Young-Bruehl's biography of Anna Freud (1988), it is made clear how, in the wake of his contemplation of his own death, Freud came to write "The theme of the three caskets" (1913f); and how he nominated Anna in a letter to Ferenczi (Freud, 1913) as successor to "my Marty–Cordelia", the term of endearment he used in his youth for his fiancée. We are seldom able to practise all we preach (". . . renounce love, choose death . . .") and Freud, as Young-Bruehl sensitively exposes, was nothing if not human.

Most tellingly of all—all, that is, from my reading—is to be found in the death of the Prince, Don Fabrizio, in Lampedusa's novel (1958) *Il Gattopardo* (*The Leopard*). Written in the certain knowledge of his own imminent death, Lampedusa declares his fantasy of the moment of death. The Prince is on his death-bed surrounded by his family, following a succession of strokes. The last rites have been administered and he is now no longer conscious. The last stroke has left him out of touch with all in his mind but for the crashing of the sea.

> Suddenly amid the group appeared a young woman; slim, in brown travelling dress and wide bustle, with a straw hat trimmed with a speckled veil which could not hide the sly charm of her face. She slid a little suede-gloved hand between one elbow and another of the weeping kneelers, apologised, drew closer. It was she, the creature for ever yearned for, coming to fetch him; strange that one so young should yield to him; the time for the train's departure must be very dose. When she was face to face with him she raised her veil, and there, chaste but ready for possession, she looked lovelier than she ever had when glimpsed in stellar space.
>
> The crashing of the sea subsided altogether.

A senile, demented man, seventy-eight, complained to his son he could not get into his home, his wife having put him in an hotel prior to abandoning him in her own despair and fear of death. His son asked why he should want to get into his home. He answered; "I have got to. I must find my mother."

I return now to examine how Shakespeare deals with Lear's struggle to revive the object, to have the object able to think of him, to forgive him, and accept him finally that he may die in peace. As we shall see the poet is true to the end. Lear will die as he lived.

LEAR: [to Cordelia] You do me wrong to take me out o'th' grave;
Thou art a soul in bliss; but I am bound
Upon a wheel of fire, that mine own tears
Do scald like tears of molten lead. (4.7: 45–48)

and

> You are a spirit, I know; where did you die? (4.7: 49)

She cannot be alive in external reality. He kneels before her, as if to mother, seeking forgiveness. But she wants her father's blessing. He is muddled as to whether she lives or not. He says:

LEAR: Pray do not mock me:
          I am a very foolish fond old man,

          . . .

          I fear I am not in my perfect mind (4.7: 59–63)

and, unsure of where he is, or whence he came,

> For, as I am a man, I think this lady
> To be my child Cordelia. (4.7: 68–69)

he attempts the confession

LEAR: . . . weep not:
          If you have poison for me, I will drink it. (4.7: 71–72)

and it comes to nothing, as I have already argued.

The doctor, warning Cordelia, says: ". . . the great rage, You see, is kill'd in him".

Later, in the charge of Edmund, Cordelia invites the thought of reconciliation with her sisters; but Lear still seeks to evade any contemplation of the frightful consequences of his rage, so necessary if he is to yield and to mourn his own life. The denial is almost unbelievable.

LEAR: No, no, no, no! Come, let's away to prison;
          We two alone will sing like birds i'th'cage: . . . (5.3: 8–9)

In denial of father, a denial implicit throughout, he will, he believes, find blissful reunion with the object, now alive for him. Not so: reality intervenes yet again. She is hanged—to remind us the object is truly dead.

LEAR: Howl, howl, howl! . . .

          . . .

          She's dead as earth . . . (5.3: 255–259)

Earth? Mother Earth?

> I might have sav'd her; now she's gone for ever!
> Cordelia, Cordelia! stay a little . . . (5.3: 268–269)

He seeks to deny her death and boasts in the same moment of his triumph at having slain her killer.

He will not have it so. She must be alive, to think of him. How else can she come and fetch him away to death. His last words:

LEAR: Do you see this? Look on her, look, her lips,
    Look there, look there! (5.3: 307–309)

And he dies.

The object is dead. It was dead and it did not come for him. He has had to die in an omnipotent pretence, his illusions preserved and taken to the grave.

Bradley (1904) supposed Lear's death to be due to the joy of thinking Cordelia was alive, after all.

Martin Lings (1984) agrees. It can only mean Cordelia is alive and so Lear dies in a state of bliss. But I suspect he comes nearer to the heart of the matter when he asks, "Can it be it was because he saw (*or thought that he saw*) that Cordelia was alive that he died?" (my italics).

My argument, then, comes down to this. There is a need to restore and repair the object, to give life to a forgiving mother, a mother capable of thinking about him, in order to yield and surrender himself to her repossession. In common parlance, to be at peace with oneself, so to "meet one's maker", and face the "Day of Judgement", tolerable only in the anticipation of forgiveness.

The infantile omnipotence upon which our survival initially depends (Symington, 1985), invokes an internalized experience of possessing a woman who possessed us (Conran, 1976). Such is the basis of what we call being self-possessed, the antithesis of madness.

Lear's death, and possibly others I have cited, refers to the reversal of this process. Self-possession is lost, yet the need to be nursed prevails and repossession entails a surrender of the self to the object in death.

LEAR: I lov'd her most, and thought to set my rest
    On her kind nursery . . . (1.1: 123–124)

Can it be that, as we are nursed into this world, on to "this great stage of fools", so are we likely to be nursed out of it? As our object relationships develop, so will they be undone?

Charles Lamb, who saw so clearly that we are Lear, reminds us that, in the end, "We are nothing, less than nothing and dreams. We are only what might have been . . ."

Summary

In this paper I have attempted to describe how a man's relationship to his internal objects may determine his approach to and acceptance of his death; and how this depends upon his capacity for self-forgiveness as he seeks reunion with the object. The capacity for self-forgiveness directly determines, it is argued, how the admission of guilt is possible, as distinct from shame, which is seen to excite the defences of denial, splitting, and projection. The distinction is made between the admission of guilt and confession, which latter is seen to be a projection. In taking the madness and death of King Lear as my example, I have sought to demonstrate how skilfully Shakespeare directs our attention to the difficulties man encounters in taking responsibility for his mental life, if he is to anticipate a peaceful and dignified exit.

Acknowledgements

I am grateful to Naomi Conran, for insisting I put pen to paper and so deepening my interest in King Lear; and to Felicity Firth and Luigi Caparrotta for their help in providing translations from the Italian of Pirandello.

Note

1. My teacher, Tom Hayward, would have spoken for him in his pre-psychotic state, saying, "It's being so mad that keeps me sane."

References

Bradley, A. C. (1904). Shakespearean Tragedy. London: Macmillan.

Champion, L. S. (1980). *King Lear: An Annotated Bibliography*. New York: Garland.

Coleridge, S. T. (1818). *Lectures and Notes on Shakespeare*. Collected by T. Ashe (1890). London: Geo. Bell & Sons.

Conran, M. B. (1976). Incestuous failure: studies of transference phenomena with young psychotic patients and their mothers. *International Journal of Psychoanalysis, 57*: 477–481.

Fairbairn, W. R. D. (1952). *Psychoanalytic Studies of the Personality*. London: Tavistock.

Freud, S. (1913f). The theme of the three caskets. *S.E., 12*: 291–301. London: Hogarth.

Freud, S. (1913). Letter to Sandor Ferenczi. In: *Letters of Sigmund Freud*, selected by Ernst L. Freud. New York: Basic Books, 1960.

Freud, S. (1920g). Beyond the pleasure principle. *S.E., 18*: 7–64. London: Hogarth.

Freud, S. (1940a). An outline of psycho-analysis. *S.E., 23*: 141–207. London: Hogarth.

Guntrip, H. (1964). *Healing the Sick Mind*. London: Unwin.

Hanly, C. (1986). Lear and his daughters. *International Review of Psychoanalysis, 13*: 211–220.

Hess, N. (1987). King Lear and some anxieties of old age. *British Institute of Medical Psychology, 60*: 209–215.

Jaques, E. (1965). Death and the mid-life crisis. *International Journal of Psychoanalysis, 46*: 502–514.

Kinston, W. (1987). The shame of narcissism. In: D. L. Nathanson (Ed.), *The Many Faces of Shame* (pp. 214–245). New York: Guilford Press.

Lamb, C. (1912). *The Complete Works*. London: Chatto and Windus.

Lambert, A. (1990). Stalin's prisoner to the end. *The Independent Weekend*, 10 March: p. 29.

Lampedusa, G. di (1960). *The Leopard*, A. Colquhoun (Trans.). London: Collins and Harvill.

Likierman, M. (1987). The function of anger in human conflict. *International Review of Psychoanalysis, 14*: 143–161.

Lings, M. (1984). *The Secret of Shakespeare*. Wellingborough Aquarian Press.

Marteau, L. (1988). Reading about pastoral psychology. *British Journal of Psychiatry, 152*: 148–149.

Pasternak, B. (1958). *Dr Zhivago*. M. Hayward & M. Harari (Trans.). London: Collins & Harvill Press.

Perelberg, R. J. (1980). Umbanda and psychoanalysis as different ways of interpreting mental illness. *British Journal of Medical Psychology, 53*: 323–332.

Pirandello, L. (1915). Colloqui coi personaggi, Sezione 2. *Giornale di Sicilia*, 11–12 settembre.

Rosenfeld, H. (1965). *Psychotic States*. London: Hogarth.

Rycroft, C. (1968). *A Critical Dictionary of Psychoanalysis*. London: Nelson.

Shakespeare, W. (1972). *King Lear: The Arden Edition*. K. Muir (Ed.). London: Methuen.

Sharpe, E. F. (1946). From *King Lear* to *The Tempest*. *International Journal of Psychoanalysis*, 27: 19–30.

Speziale-Bagliacca, R. (1980). Lear, Cordelia, Kent and the Foci: A psychoanalytic interpretation. *International Review of Psychoanalysis*, 7: 413–428.

Steiner, J. (1982). Perverse relationships between parts of the self. *International Journal of Psychoanalysis*, 63: 241–251.

Symington, J. (1985). The survival function of primitive omnipotence. *International Journal of Psychoanalysis*, 66: 481–487.

Thubron, C. (1987). *Behind the Wall*. London: Heinemann.

Winnicott, D. W. (1955). The depressive position in normal emotional development. *British Journal of Medical Psychology*, 28: 88–100.

Yorke, C. (1989). Personal communication.

Young-Bruehl, E. (1989). *Anna Freud*. London: Macmillan.

CHAPTER FIVE

The other side of the wall. A psychoanalytic study of creativity in later life*

Peter Hildebrand

I wish to address myself in this chapter to the notion of creativity in later life. I do not intend to do more than briefly summarize the classical view of creativity as put forward originally by Sigmund Freud and developed by other psychoanalysts over the past eighty years. I wish instead to bring together several strands of thought arising from consideration of object-relations theory and the application of structuralist ideas to psychoanalytic thinking, together with recent interest in the developmental stages of later life. I will combine this approach with a critique of certain notions put forward by René Major in his work on *Hamlet* and apply the amended theory to an outstanding creative work of later life: William Shakespeare's last complete play *The Tempest*.

The Tempest, although the last complete play written by Shakespeare, is accorded pride of place in the Folio of 1623. Subsequent to its presentation at Court in 1612 on the occasion of the marriage

---

*This paper was delivered by invitation at the Anglo-French Colloquium on "Creativity and Psychoanalysis", organized by the Ambassade de France in London in April 1986. © Institute of Psychoanalysis, London.

of the Winter Queen, Elizabeth of Bohemia, Shakespeare seems to have retired to Stratford, where he lived with his married daughter and her husband at New Place until his death some four years later.

The play is in the form of a romantic comedy and contains a masque, or a play within a play. It recounts the events of a few hours when the galleon carrying Alonso, King of Naples and his retinue sails near the island where Prospero, once Duke of Milan, and his daughter Miranda are living in exile. Using magic arts, Prospero conjures up a storm and creates the illusion that the ship has been cast ashore. With the aid of his familiar spirit, Ariel, he achieves a situation that enables him to regain his Dukedom, to marry his daughter to the King's son, and redress the wrongs he has suffered at the hands of his usurping brother. This bald summary gives no indication of the subtlety and beauty of the play and the intricacy of much of the verse, which has made it one of the best loved and perhaps most misunderstood of Shakespeare's plays.

I take it as a given that any psychoanalytic theory of creativity needs to account for such mature work in creative artists as well as relating them to their early productions. Freud said, "In the exercising of an art, it [psychoanalysis] sees once again an activity intended to allay ungratified wishes—in the first place in the creative artist himself and subsequently in his audience or spectators" (Freud, 1913–1914, p. 187). In Elizabeth Wright's view, Freud suggested that the writer produces a surrogate neurosis, which incited both a public (cathartic) transferential relationship as well as a private one (Wright, 1984). This is a view that has been developed by a number of writers, notably Chasseguet-Smirgel, who has developed her own version of classical psychoanalytic theory concerning creativity. While acknowledging the importance and fruitfulness of the classical psychoanalytic tradition and its roots in biological theory, I am always struck by the parallel between this type of approach to psychological phenomena and the economic theories of the modern Tory Party in Great Britain. Just as everything in Mrs Thatcher's views seems to be reduced to the notions of financial probity and good management typified by her family's corner shop in Grantham, I sometimes feel that everything in classical theory must be reduced to drive derivatives. Thus, Chasseguet-Smirgel says

Creation has a function that goes further than that of sublimation. In fact, it is a matter of using the sublimated creative act to gain access to one's integrity by passing through a spectrum of sublimated impulse discharges . . . The creative act is an attempt to achieve integrity, to overcome castration at every level. [1984, p. 404]

While I have no wish to minimize the importance of psychosexual factors in our understanding of creative work in human beings, one has to recall that Freud himself laid down his arms before the problem of creativity at a time when psychosexual factors were central to his thinking and that he maintained, wrongly as we now know, that after the age of forty people became too fixed and rigid in their cognitive patterns to be amenable to analysis or psychic change and development. Plainly we need an extended theory to account for certain creative productions in later life. Moreover, I suspect that I am not alone in finding the classical approach unsatisfying, whatever its attractions in terms of simplicity and heuristic value. Personally, I prefer complexity and subtlety, and feel that of all human attributes, the capacity to create works of art fashioned through symbolic representation is perhaps the most human and the most complicated.

In this chapter, therefore, I shall present a series of rather disjunctive thoughts as a way of approaching the problem of later-life creativity and throwing a different, personal, though in no way more "profound", light on the topic. Thus, object-relations theorists in Great Britain have refused to assume that the unconscious is merely a cauldron of seething excitement and have underlined a basic unconscious human need to maintain meaningful contact with others. Thus, Rycroft (1985) states that "man is innately a symbolizing animal who generates meanings whenever he acts" (p. 342).

Rycroft continues:

By assuming, as Freud did in his theoretical writings but not always in his clinical papers, that the unconscious, the id, was "a chaos, a cauldron of seething excitement . . . which was a slave to the pleasure principle and neglected the reality of the external world" and had therefore to be repressed, modified and organized before an integrated, rational and realistic ego could develop, Freud was, it seemed—and still seems—to me, taking an intellectualist, antiemotional stance. By describing unconscious mental processes as primitive, archaic, irrational and unrealistic and attributing to the healthy ego a rational, objective state of mind which is in fact that of a scientist or professional man while at work and that of an ordinary, healthy human being at home, at play or in love, he ensnared his theory in a paradox, to which most of his followers have loyally accommodated themselves: the effect of psychoanalytical treatment is to create personalities which embrace just those emotional, imaginative elements that its theoretical conception of a rational ego excludes (*ibid.*, p. 122).

Rycroft resolves the paradox in the following way:

This is that human behaviour is actuated not only by the need to satisfy instinctual impulses but also by the need to maintain meaningful contact with others—that, as Susanne Langer herself put it, "human behaviour is not only a food-getting strategy, but is also a language . . . every move is at the same time a gesture". Another way of putting this is to say that man is innately a symbolizing animal who generates meanings whenever he acts.

According to Susanne Langer there are two types of symbolism available for expressing and communicating meanings: discursive symbolism, which is language as the term is ordinarily understood, i.e. words with fixed meanings arranged in series according to agreed rules, and non-discursive symbolism, in which images are presented simultaneously and derive their meaning from their context in the total pattern. In *The Innocence of Dreams* I have argued that dreaming is an intrapsychic communicative activity using non-discursive symbolism and that the "primary" processes—condensation, displacement and symbolization—which Freud discovered to be characteristic of dreaming, are the figures of speech of a non-discursive language which uses images, particularly bodily images, as its vocabulary and sources of metaphor. Such a view of the matter implies, of course, an agent, a self who is more than our usual waking state, who generates meanings, sends messages and constructs dreams and symptoms, and it regards dreams not as "mental phenomena" that we sometimes observe but as expressive activities to which we sometimes listen. [*ibid.*, p. 124]

Clearly this argument can also be related to the creative act as well.

I wish to add to this object-relations hypothesis of a fundamental world of unconscious meanings that is as fundamental an unconscious structure as the id, a structural hypothesis (Kuper,

1986). Kuper considers that an understanding of the work of Lévi-Strauss and his "logic of the concrete" (Lévi-Strauss, 1962), is crucial to the understanding of dreams and creativity. This was a mode of thought that constituted symbolic objects in terms of a set of binary oppositions, and combined these constructs for messages. Lévi-Strauss assumes that a mental structure, typically a myth, formulates its message along two dimensions. One—the metaphoric dimension—involves selection of items from a series of binary oppositions (such as male/female, up/down, hot/cold, young/old). The other, the combinatory dimension, has to do with the organization of these items in series, syntagmatic chains. The combinatory sequences are less strictly limited than the selective choices, but they are also constrained by transformation rules. Once a particular situation has been specified in a myth, the movement forward is achieved through formal transformations, in which the items are inverted, reversed, negated, etc.

Consider the opening sequences of four North American myths about bird-nesters, discussed in the final volume of his *Mythologiques* (1981). Each of these "overtures" (as Lévi-Strauss calls them, exploiting his own favourite analogy between primitive myth and classical European music) features a hero and one of three female relatives. The first hero has a sister, who is protective; the second a grandmother, who tries to commit incest with him; and the third, a cannibalistic mother. In the fourth myth the hero is confronted with all three female relatives, but their attributes are juggled. In this myth, the sister is incestuous, the grandmother cannibalistic, and the mother protective. In other words, the three female relatives are defined in terms of three contrasting feminine attributes, which are systematically rotated. Each female character appears twice in this set of four myths. On each appearance she has a different label (incestuous, protective, or cannibalistic). Moreover, in no myth are two of these women given the same label. This set of three defining attributes may itself be reduced to two sets of oppositions—tabooed *vs.* permitted behaviour, and sexual *vs.* culinary regulations.

The women are also further contrasted in terms of another cluster of symbols that oppose: menstruating women, pregnant women, and post-menopausal women. These attributes are more obviously mutually exclusive. Menstruating women cannot be pregnant, pregnant women cannot menstruate, and post-menopausal women can neither menstruate nor become pregnant. These qualities in turn refer to culturally more fundamental oppositions, between youth and age, fertility and sterility, birth and death. They also tie in with ideas about the phases of the moon.

By specifying these basic oppositions, the myths arm themselves with the means by which they are able to communicate culturally resonant messages.

Kuper then suggests that while the binary oppositions are rather rigid and mechanical, the transformations of mythical constructions are comparatively free.

> Theoretically, at least, there is no limit to the possible number of transformations . . . from the purely theoretical point of view, there is no way of deriving . . . any principle from which it would follow that the states of the group are necessarily finite in number . . . [Kuper, 1986, p. 41]

And yet, transformations seem to follow certain rules. Lévi-Strauss believes that this points to the existence of further mental universals:

> If, between one variant and another of the same myth, there always appear differences expressible, not in the form of small positive or negative increments, but of clear-cut relationships such as contrariness, contradiction, inversion of symmetry, this is because the "transformational" aspect is not the whole story: some other principle must come into play to determine that only some of the possible states of the myth are actualized, and that only certain apertures, not all, are opened up in the grid which, theroetically, could accommodate any number. This additional constraint results from the fact that the mind, which is working unconsciously on the mythic substance, has at its disposal only mental procedures of a certain type. [Lévi-Strauss, 1981, pp. 675–676]

The next step in my argument is to suggest that psychoanalysis needs to acknowledge that we organize our creative and imaginative life through both psychosexual and non-discursive meanings: and, moreover, that we all have individual grids of meanings that can be thought of as having the same structures as myths. In this sense we constantly create and recreate our personal and unique myths from the raw stuff of our existence through the medium of our dreams, neuroses, and creative work. Moreover, creativity is a lifelong process, which may find differing expression at different developmental phases in the life of any given individual. I think it likely that *mature* creativity in later life may well transmute and express earlier infantile and adolescent themes in a more ego-syntonic and satisfactory way than earlier theorists have suggested. The form that this may take may well be more fragmentary and allusive than earlier works, and yet carry a greater charge of meaning than the more structured works that the individual has produced earlier in his or her life. An excellent example would be the late watercolours of Cézanne.

I would like to bring together, at this point, the notions of Elliott Jaques (1965), with whose basic tenet concerning the universality of a midlife crisis at the age of thirty-seven I cannot agree, but whose notion of different types of creativity at different times of life, i.e., hot from the fire creativity in youth *vs* sculptured creativity in later life, I find sympathetic; and George Pollock (1982), who, in his various papers on creativity in later life, has made very convincingly the point that later life work has to do with mourning for one's own losses and the transmutation of these through creative processes as one ages. I hold that there are grounds for suggesting that as well as there being primal fantasies concerning birth and the primal scene there are also primal fantasies concerning one's own death, and that these often become central to and are expressed in many ways in the creative work of artists, particularly as they age (Hildebrand, 1985, 1987).

I would like to turn now to the work of a French colleague that seems to me to be of importance to this area of creativity: René Major's paper entitled "Names: proper and improper" (Major, 1985). In this paper, Major analyses *Hamlet* in terms of a psychoanalytic theory of proper names, and says,

> Proper names distinguish one person from another. The proper name is thus a mark without meaning (an unmeaning mark) . . . insignificant and yet remarkable, in both senses of the word. It allows us to recognize someone, but the mark can be used more than once and even endlessly. The mark is valid at the time for one person and for all those who have the same name. This produces homonymy; names which have no relationship (in terms of what they designate) may coincide. As far as proper names are

concerned coincidence may just as well make them homonymous.
[*ibid*., p. 9]

Using terms derived from Antonin Artaud, Major designates the
theatre as a place "where transference makes itself felt through
excess". Major's notion is that the proper name is the medium
through which—in classical theatre—transference effects itself. As
he says,

> The nomination and exchange of names assures the reproduction of
> representation, but the necessary split in representation introduced
> by repression takes place between desire and death. With *Hamlet*
> (which Freud considers to be the first modern play) it becomes
> *exemplary*. [*ibid*.]

He claims that in *Hamlet* the use of proper names carries a challenge
of signification which enables us, the audience, to understand the
psychological transferences that are going on on the stage. He
points out that Hamlet has to believe the ghost who, at the beginning of the play, may be no more than a projection of his own
fantasies. In order to convince himself and to convince one important other—Horatio—Hamlet has to stage a play within a play.

> Hamlet has the actors perform The Dumb-Show, the mime, and
> then the play which reproduces the scene in which a character
> pours poison into the ear of the sleeping King. But the pantomime
> only tells the "argument" of the piece. It doesn't reveal its secret.
> The latter must be uttered. "The players cannot keep counsel;
> they'll tell all." Nonetheless, producing the play within the play is
> not enough. From being an actor, the tragedy's King (Claudius) has
> become a spectator. And in so far as he is a spectator, he knows that
> the player-king doesn't die. He can remain impassive. Claudius
> might have shown no particular distress if what I call a practicable
> in French—a linking dialogue—had not taken place between
> Hamlet and himself, interrupting the unfolding of the play. Their
> dialogue bears essentially on the title of the piece and the name of
> the characters. The title: The Mousetrap. The subject: a murder
> committed in Vienna. Claudius does not know that Hamlet knows
> that he is the murderer of his father. The court in attendance for the
> performance know nothing, nor does the Queen. These are all
> things the audience know. For Hamlet, the nub is to make it known

that he knows through making manifest in Claudius the uneasiness which will prove to him that what he knows is accurate and will assure him that from that moment on Claudius will be certain that he knows. To get to that point, there is only one means available: to get the names of the one play to pass over into the other. Hamlet replies to Claudius' questions: "Gonzago is the duke's name; his wife, Baptista". Lucianus is the character who pours poison into Gonzago's ear; "the story is extant, and writ in choice Italian". "You shall see anon", Hamlet announces, "how the murderer gets the love of Gonzago's wife". With these words, whereby Claudius and Lucianus become equivalent, the king rises and leaves the show. An unusual situaton: a spectator, who has come to the theatre to live an imaginary life, there finds a representation of his real life. [*ibid.*, pp. 11]

Please keep these words in mind when we consider *The Tempest*. Major goes on to say:

Through the play of proper names which the Italian play introduces, the scenes become interchangeable. To the extent that Gonzago represents the old King Hamlet, Claudius, occupying Lucianus' place, may end up in Gonzago's place if Prince Hamlet, the nephew of Claudius, becomes the homonym of Lucianus, Gonzago's nephew. All the dramatic force of the piece consists in the fact that names that have no relationship come to coincide with one another. If one adds to the chessboard the death of Shakespeare's father around the time of the writing of Hamlet and the name of Shakespeare's son, Hamnet, dead at an early age, the circle is closed, running from Shakespeare's son to the play's spectator, identified with the Prince who dies by the poisoned sword. Across the centuries, Shakespeare continues to bring his son to life, in each of us. [*ibid.*, p. 12]

The name of Hamlet renders those of Gonzago, of King Hamlet, and of Claudius homonymic. Even though they have no relationship with each other, it makes them coincide. With the name Hamlet—this is also true for Oedipus—there is an end to a dynasty, which gives these names an exceptional significance.

Let me try to summarize my argument up to this point. I suggest that in the theatre the proper names chosen for the characters will convey not only something about them, but also reflect significations that are part of the dramatist's own personal myth, as well as reverberating through both the spectator's external world and his inner personal nexus of meanings. I would add that *Hamlet*, in particular, because it so clearly and yet so densely treats the themes of oedipal rivalry between sons and fathers, the desire for the mother, guilt, and the whole question of denomination and identity in a doubly theatrical way, i.e., the play, the play within the play, the play within the spectator, has always been paradigmatic for the psychoanalyst to consider and understand.

Bearing these very different strands of my argument in mind in considering *The Tempest*, I will assume a reasonable knowledge of the plot and characters and treat specifically some hitherto unaddressed aspects of the work. Jan Kott (1967) says

> Shakespeare's dramas are constructed not on the principle of unity of action, but on the principle of analogy, comprising a double, treble or quadruple plot, which repeats the same basic theme; they are a system of mirrors both concave and convex which reflect, magnify and parody the same situation. [*ibid.*, p. 72]

I am suggesting that the same notion can be applied across the Shakespearian canon. After all, Henry James, no mean authority when it comes to ghost stories, called *Hamlet* the *central reflector*! My thesis is that indeed *Hamlet* represented certain oedipal themes that Shakespeare worked and reworked throughout his life, and that in this, his last major work, *The Tempest*, he returns to the themes of succession, usurpation, identity, and retribution in order to work them through once again. Because it is a romance, the play is not ostensibly about the tragic aspects of these themes, but to my mind they are linked as closely to the themes of *Hamlet* as is manifest content to latent content.

The Tempest is a play deeply concerned with magic. It centres around the arrival near the island of exile of Prospero, former Duke of Milan, of a galleon carrying *inter alia* Alonso, King of Naples and his son Fernando, his brother Sebastian, Antonio the usurping Duke of Milan and brother to Prospero and Gonzalo, honest old counsellor to the King. Prospero, rightful Duke of Milan, has been cast adrift to die with his infant daughter Miranda, but they and his magic books are saved thanks to the care and mercy of Gonzalo. He has since lived in isolation on the island with his spirit Ariel, whom he had freed from imprisonment by the now dead witch Sycorax, and also with her son Caliban, a monster who wishes to ravish Miranda and has rejected Prospero's attempts to civilize him. Nevertheless, Caliban can understand and respond to beauty, although he is overtly sexual and aggressive—like the rest of mankind.[1]

The play opens when the ship carrying the King of Naples and his retinue is apparently wrecked by a magical storm conjured up by Prospero. When Miranda pities those drowned, Prospero's first words are, "Be collected. No more amazement. Tell your piteous heart there's no harm done".

MIRANDA: O, woe the day!
PROSPERO: No harm. (1.2: 14–15)

I think these words are significant beyond their immediate meaning. Prospero's signature in the play is immediately set. There is to be no harm done. This is not to be a tragedy of blood and revenge and, despite the supernatural elements that will shortly appear, there is to be no parricide or ghostly paternal apparition on this stage. Prospero's speech continues:

> I have done nothing but in care of thee,
> Of thee, my dear one, thee my daughter, who
> Art ignorant of what thou art, naught knowing
> Of whence I am, nor that I am more better
> Than Prospero, master of a full poor cell.
> And thy no greater father. (1.2: 16–21)

Prospero now asks Miranda to pluck his magic garment from him, "So, lie there, my art", and proceeds to tell her a non-illusory truth about their joint identities. His concern is with daughters and the succession—a theme hardly surprising for a writer who has one daughter married to a successful and well-trusted physician and another daughter still to be married. Shakespeare's father and son are both long dead—but daughters do not need to be deceived.

PROSPERO: . . . Wipe thou thine eyes. Have comfort.
          The direful spectacle of the wrack, which touched
          The very virtue of compassion in thee.
          I have with such provision in mine art

> So safely ordered, that there is no soul—
> No, not so much perdition as an hair
> Betid to any creature in the vessel
> Which thou heard'st cry, which thou saw'st sink.
> (1.2: 25–32)

The Tempest is a romance. Prospero's care for his daughter and his deliberate lack of malice are at once established. The audience are shown that they have been the objects of a non-malicious theatrical illusion and that the ship and its passengers have survived. Yet no one can be sure what is illusion and what is truth in this magical matter—rather like the quest for truth at the opening of *Hamlet*. The meanings slide over one another. Prospero now suggests finding the roots of these events in the past, "What seest thou else in the dark backward and abysm of time?", and uses Miranda's childhood memories to demonstrate that he is the true Duke of Milan (writ in choice Italian). Her natural question is "What foul play had we, that we came from there?" Prospero tells her that his brother has seized the city while they slept ("O my prophetic soul, my Uncle!") "I pray thee mark me that a brother should be so perfidious". He has *usurped* the throne while Prospero has been absorbed in the study of his magic arts. But thanks to the old nobleman Gonzalo, who has secretly preserved them, they have landed on the island and Prospero has developed his magic powers.

The name Gonzalo is absolutely crucial to my argument here. I consider that the homonym Gonzalo/Gonzago provides the *practicable*—the unconscious link between the two plays of *Hamlet* and *The Tempest*—and signifies for us that the later piece represents a different age-specific treatment of some of the major themes of the earlier play. For example, it is now revealed to us that Prospero, as well as being a magician, can employ a familiar spirit called Ariel, who has separated the King's son, Ferdinand, from the other members of the crew whom he has cast into an enchanted sleep. After a brief entry to establish Caliban and his fury and hatred of Prospero, and his wish to rape Miranda, Ferdinand enters, together with Ariel, who is invisible to Ferdinand, and says,

FERDINAND: . . . Sitting on a bank,
          Weeping again the King my father's wrack,

This music crept by me upon the waters,
Allaying both their fury and my passion
With its sweet air. Thence I have followed it,
Or it hath drawn me, rather. But t'is gone
No, it begins again. (1.2: 193–199)

This is followed by Ariel's beautiful song "Full fathom five thy father lies". In a most extraordinary and haunting echo of Hamlet's scene upon the battlements, Ferdinand says "The ditty does remember my drowned father. This is no mortal business, nor no sound that the earth owes". But it is not the comrades of the watch on the battlements who are the spectators, but Prospero and Miranda, who falls in love immediately with Ferdinand, the first young man whom she has ever seen. Prospero watches the scene with pleasure, confirms their mutual infatuation and then says to Ferdinand, who now believes that he has succeeded his father as King and wishes to offer this new found kingdom to Miranda: "One word more I charge that thee that thou attend me. Thou do'st here *usurp the name* thou own'st not" (my italics); i.e., challenging his claim that he has now become the King.

Prospero gives Ferdinand menial tasks to do in order to confirm the love of the two young people, while the scene changes. And what is fascinating here is that Gonzalo, whom I have nominated as the "practicable", acts as the animator of the next and most significant scene in which Alonzo, Sebastian, Antonio, and he take part. After Alonzo has expressed grief for the supposed loss of his son, Gonzalo presents us with his picture of a Golden Age—an idealized fantasy that may make up for what is the insupportable loss of an adult child (Hildebrand, 1985), until, under the spell of Ariel, all fall asleep except for Sebastian and Antonio, who discuss the possibility of Sebastian usurping the Kingdom of Naples. Antonio works Sebastian up:

ANTONIO: . . . There be that can rule Naples as well as he that
sleeps: lords that can prate as amply and unnecessarily
as this Gonzalo. I myself could make a chough of as
deep chat. O, that you bore the mind that I do! What a
sleep were this for your advancement! Do you
understand me?
SEBASTIAN: Methinks I do.

ANTONIO: And how does your content tender your own good
            fortune?
SEBASTIAN: You did supplant your brother Prospero.
ANTONIO: True. And look how well my garments sit upon me,
            Much feater than before. My brother's servants were
            then my fellows. Now they are my men.
SEBASTIAN: But, for your conscience?
ANTONIO: Ay, sir, where lies that? If 'twere a kibe,
            'Twould put me to my slipper; but I feel not
            This deity in my bosom. Twenty consciences
            That stand 'twixt me and Milan, candied be they,
            And melt ere they molest. Here lies your brother,
            No better than the earth he lies upon,
            If he were that which now he's like—that's dead—
            Whom I with this obedient steel, three inches of it,
            Can lay to bed for ever; whiles you, doing thus . . .
            (2.1: 267–289)

They are just about to kill the King and his companions *as they
sleep* when Ariel enters and awakens the sleepers. The whole scene
has been orchestrated by Prospero, so that we, like Claudius in
Hamlet, think we are going to see an innocent play, until we are
forced to realize our own complicity in the piece. The parallel with
The Mousetrap—the play within the play—where we are shown
Hamlet the Dane, who is sleeping in his orchard when he is
murdered by his brother, who then takes his Kingdom and his wife
and usurps the throne, is phenomenal. But unlike Claudius, we
cannot leap to our feet and cry for torches—we needs must watch,
and watch again while the tragedy of usurpation is played again as
tragi-comedy by Caliban, and the drunkards. Prospero, on his
island is showing the world to Miranda, and of course, us to
ourselves—our follies, our sexual infatuations, and our illusions.
While Hamlet poses the question "Who am I?", we are asked "Who
are you?"

Let us leave *The Tempest* for a moment while Shakespeare works
out his plot, and look further at some elements of myth that seem
common to *Hamlet* and *The Tempest*. We find the rivalry between the
good and wicked brothers; the murder of the king while sleeping
contrasted with the preservation of the king while sleeping; the

supernatural appearance of the dead king *vs.* the supernatural appearance of the supposedly dead king; the ruler is murdered and demands revenge *vs.* the ruler is threatened with murder but forgoes revenge. The themes here are greed, envy, desire, contrasted with loving kindness, trust, and generativity both within and between generations. I suggest that without the addition of these basic meaningful relationships analysed in structuralist terms, any psychoanalytic interpretation must remain incomplete. With them the work of art carries more effect for the reader or spectator, in the sense that the meanings are multi-layered and convey multiple resonances of this particular myth.

So we can identify with and enjoy the irony of Miranda's comment when she exclaims on meeting the King and his retinue of villains and would-be murderers for the first time,

MIRANDA: Oh, wonder,
How many goodly creatures are there here!
How beauteous mankind is! Oh brave new world
that has such people in't!

To which Prospero replies, "'Tis new to thee".

While we are aware of the writer's irony and our own scepticism, since we think we know who they are—despite the fact that Miranda, as spectator, may be observing us who think that we are spectators but are of course as much embedded in the drama through our own transferences as are the actors themselves—it nevertheless seems plausible to suggest here that Shakespeare may be using the piece to work out his problem of generativity and renunciation by and through each of us.

Such an approach would speak against Major's notion that the doomed dynasty of the Hamlets *denominates* itself in death. Moreover, in the companion case of Oedipus this is certainly not true, since, by the manner of his death, Oedipus donates his generativity to the Athenian state. If *The Tempest* does indeed represent a reworking of the same themes, then the message is that power can be handed on if it is relinquished voluntarily and accepted neither enviously or greedily but worked and sacrificed for.

I must also discuss the two magic appearances in Acts 3 and 4, where first we have the mime of presenting and then removing the spectral banquet to the King and Court, in the course of which Ariel accuses Alonso of complicity in Prospero's exile and the King acknowledges his guilt and states what he considers to be the appropriate punishment.

ALONSO: Therefore my son with ooze is bedded, and
           I'll sink him deeper than e'er plummet sounded,
           And with him there lie mudded. (3.3: 1090–102)

This is an extraordinary evocation of Hamnet Shakespeare, whose death and burial in the churchyard of Stratford church are recorded in the Parish register for 1596. To this day the churchyard lies hard by the water meadows of the Avon, and the reference is surely to the loss of an adult child (Hamnet was nearly twelve) which, as I have shown elsewhere, it is never really possible to accept and work through (Hildebrand, 1985).

This episode is followed by the Ceres masque presented to Ferdinand and Miranda, which leads Ferdinand to say,

           Let me live here for ever!
           So rare a wondered father and a wise
           Makes this place Paradise. (4.1: 21–23)

But the villains now break in.

Most commentators on the The Tempest have suggested that Shakespeare has used Prospero as his voice in the marvellous speech in Act 4 in which he says to Ferdinand:

PROSPERO: . . . Be cheerful, Sir
           Our revels now are ended. These our actors,
           As I foretold you, were all spirits, and
           Are melted into air, into thin air;
           And, like the baseless fabric of this vision,
           The cloud capped towers, the gorgeous palaces,
           The solemn temples, the great globe itself,
           Yea, all which it inherit, shall dissolve,
           And, like this insubstantial pageant faded,
           Leave not a wrack behind. We are such stuff
           As dreams are made on; and our little life
           Is rounded with a sleep . . . (4.1: 147–158)

Usually they suggest that the speech marks his farewell to the stage. Apart from the fact that he contributed considerable chunks of *Henry VIII* some years later, I don't see either Shakespeare or Prospero in such a sentimental way. Prospero is a realist, and is saying that you cannot cope with evil, with drunkenness, with sexuality, without tenderness and compassion by means of *illusion*. While illusion has been enormously powerful in his exile, it is in the end theatre. Something else needs to be done in reality and he will do it by bringing the villains under control. They have spoiled the illusion and must be punished—this is the penalty that you pay for ignoring them.

Prospero is under no illusion himself about the situation that he is handing over. If the exile on the island has been his withdrawal into study and magic arts, he must now return to reality ("my every third thought shall be of death"), and he now finally releases Ariel—the Imaginary is transformed at last into the Symbolic, reluctantly but for good. He returns to Milan and to the humdrum daily round. That this may be a disaster is, of course, a danger that he cannot ignore, but if he wants to hand on the succession to Miranda and Ferdinand this, in reality, is the only choice that he can make. Acceptance of one's own mortality is the life-giving choice that will secure the dynasty. Nothing could be harder-headed than Prospero's choice—nothing further from the holocaust at the end of *Hamlet*. Where Major speaks of the "denomination of Hamlet", perhaps we should speak of the "nomination" of the children who are to succeed and who are to make their way at whatever cost to themselves.

Shakespeare, of course, has one more trick up his sleeve—we are not to get off lightly. In the Epilogue, Prospero says,

PROSPERO: Now my charms are all o'erthrown,
　　　　　　And what strength I have's mine own,
　　　　　　Which is most faint. Now 'tis true
　　　　　　I must here be confined by you,
　　　　　　Or sent to Naples. Let me not
　　　　　　Since I have my dukedom got
　　　　　　And pardoned the deceiver, dwell
　　　　　　In this bare island by your spell;
　　　　　　But release me from my bands
　　　　　　With the help of your good hands
　　　　　　Gentle breath of yours my sails

must fill, or else my project fails,
Which was to please. Now I want
Spirits to enforce, art to enchant;
And my ending is despair,
Unless I be relieved by prayer,
Which pierces so, that it assaults
mercy itself, and frees all faults.
As you from crimes would pardoned be,
Let your indulgence set me free. (Epilogue: 1–20)

The Editor of the Penguin *Tempest* says, "The superior know-ledge possessed by the theatrical audience does not pluck the heart of mystery out of Prospero's masque. It merely leads into an appear-ance–reality dilemma more profound and much more complex than the one actually perceived by the characters on the stage". When Prospero addresses himself to the audience, he may well be said to be anticipating those French analysts and literary historians who "deconstruct" by some four hundred years. The question being asked is "Who has constructed the play?" Are Prospero, Caliban, Alonso and the rest illusions of the audience or only of Shakespeare? Whose life is ending and who is facing death? Is it the play which comes to an end or is it the life which each member of the audience will have to create for himself outside the revels which have created a temporary island of refuge from reality? Prospero has been created by the response of the audience to the play-now he and they must return home. The audience's prayers are now the source of magical power-like Ariel, Prospero must pray them to release him. If they refuse, he must live in an illusion, but they cannot be free. So to be free they have to give the magic and the illusion up. Hamlet the Dane dies, and we are purged with pity and sorrow. Horatio says ". . . Good night, Sweet Prince". Prospero asks us, where shall we all lay our heads tomorrow?

I will conclude by saying that I have felt most inadequate to the task that I have set myself. I have tried to comment on the phenom-enon of late-life creativity through a work of art, and I fear that the complexity and subtlety of the task have been beyond me. Fortunately, a great modern English poet was fascinated by *The Tempest*, and it is good that I can give him the last word. This is to be found in the opening poem ("Stage manager to the critics") from

W. H. Auden's poetic response to *The Tempest* entitled *The Sea and the Mirror* (Auden, 1944).

The aged catch their breath,
For the nonchalant couple go
Waltzing across the tightrope
As if there were no death
Or hope of falling down;
The wounded cry as the clown
doubles his meaning, and O
How the dear little children laugh
When the drums roll and the lovely
Lady is sawn in half.
O what authority gives
Existence its surprise
Science is happy to answer
That the ghosts who haunt our lives
Are handy with mirrors and wire,
That song and sugar and fire,
Courage and come-hither eyes
Have a genius for taking pains.
But how does one think up a habit?
Our wonder, our terror remains.
Art opens the fishiest eye
To the flesh and the Devil who heat
The Chamber of Temptation
Where heroes roar and die.
We are wet with sympathy now;
Thanks for the evening: but how
Shall we satisfy when we meet,
Between Shall-I and I-Will,
The lions mouth whose hunger
No metaphors can fill?
Well, who in his own backyard
Has not opened his heart to the smiling
Secret he cannot quote?
Which goes to show that the Bard
Was sober when he wrote
That this world of fact we love

Is unsubstantial stuff:
All the rest is silence
On the other side of the wall;
And the silence ripeness,
And the ripeness all. [*ibid.*, pp. 3–4]

I am pleased that I discovered Auden's poetic cycle in the course of the reading that I have done for this chapter. His poem suggests a different kind of "practicable"—the link between the understanding of two great poets about the eventual impossibility of illusion to hold back and deny the reality of death. Creativity is not just about life, it is about death as well. His near contemporary, Rowe, reports of Shakespeare, that,

> The latter part of his life was spent, as all men of good sense will wish theirs may be, in ease, retirement, and the conversation of his friends. He has the good fortune to gather an estate equal to his occasion, and, in that, to his wish; and is said to have spent some years before his death at his native Stratford. [Rowe, 1709, quoted in Schoenbaum, 1975, p. 279]

Perhaps Shakespeare's greatest achievement late in life was to be able to give up the need to deal with his inner world through illusion. May we all have such good fortune before we, too, discover what is on "the other side of the wall".

Note

1. I greatly regret that the exigencies of time in the original paper did not allow me to devote sufficient space to Caliban. The interested reader is referred to Frank Kermode's introduction to the *Arden Shakespeare* (1964). All quotations are from the *Arden*.

References

Auden, W. H. (1944). *The Sea and the Mirror, A Commentary on Shakespeare's* The Tempest. A. Kirsch (Ed.). Princeton, NJ: Oxford University Press, reprinted 2003.

Chasseguet-Smirgel, J. (1984). Thoughts on the concept of reparation and the hierarchy of creative acts. *International Journal of Psychoanalysis, 11*: 399–406.

Freud, S. (1913–1914). The claims of psychoanalysis to scientific interest. *Totem and Taboo and Other Works. S.E., 13*.

Hildebrand, H. P. (1985). Object loss and development in the second half of life. In: C. Colarusso & R. Nemiroff (Eds.), *The Race Against Time* (pp. 211–226). New York: Plenum.

Hildebrand, H. P. (1987). Psychoanalysis and aging. *Chicago Annual of Psychoanalysis: 15*: 113–125.

Jaques, E. (1965). Death and the mid-life crisis. *International Journal of Psychoanalysis, 46*: 502–514.

Kott, J. (1967). *Shakespeare, Our Contemporary*. London: Methuen.

Kuper, A. (1986). Structural anthropology and the psychology of dreams. *Journal of Mind Behaviour, 7*: 2–3.

Lévi-Strauss, C. (1962). *Structural Anthropology*. New York: Basic Books.

Lévi-Strauss, C. (1981). *The Naked Man: Introduction to a Science of Mythology, Volume 4*. London: Cape.

Major, R. (1985). Names: proper and improper. Invited Address, ICA, London.

Pollock, G. (1982). The mourning-liberation process and creativity. *Chicago Annual of Psychoanalysis, 10*: 333–353.

Rycroft, C. (1985). *Psychoanalysis and Beyond*. London: Hogarth.

Schoenbaum, S. (1975). *William Shakespeare, A Compact Documentary Life*. New York: Oxford University Press.

Shakespeare, W. *The Arden Shakespeare: Complete Works*. Arden.

Wright, E. (1984). *Psychoanalytic Criticism: Theory in Practice*. London: Methuen.

CHAPTER SIX

Prospero's book

Peter Hildebrand

I n his Introduction to the discussion on the links between philosophy, literary criticism, and psychoanalysis at the Estates Generaux of Psychoanalysis in Paris in July 2000, Sergio Benvenuto claimed that

> it is not possible to establish a scientific psychology of the inner world, but only of the public world which explains why, while the philosophers have engaged with Freud and Lacan, they have never discussed Klein, Winnicott and Bion, so that their paths have diverged.

Using Benvenuto's terms, it seems to me that object relations theory is concerned with an inner world that we can know only inferentially: therefore it must be essentially hermeneutic—*belonging to or concerned with interpretation*, as the *Oxford English Dictionary* defines it—as of course is literary criticism. We may comment from a psychoanalytic viewpoint on a literary production that is of itself not an account of a lived life but an interpretation of behaviour seen through the distorting lens of the internal and external theatre of the author—Jan Kott (1967) describes *Hamlet* as "the central reflector"—but our comment must always remain an interpretation and no more. I would not go so far as Shoshana Felman when she suggests that "literature, fiction, is the only meeting place between madness and Philosophy" (Felman, 1982), but I feel that Winnicott has a point when he suggests that where literature and analysis converge is in the moment of overlap between the two—the *potential* space of play that Winnicott defined as follows:

> play is in fact neither a matter of inner psychic reality nor a matter of external reality. The place where cultural experience is located is in the *potential* space between the individual and the environment. [Winnicott, 1971, p. 118]

When we enter such a potential space in thinking about and working with our patients, when this in its turn can be related in the mind of both the analyst and/or the patient to such lived cultural experience as a play or a film, then the combination of these two hermeneutics offer us the potentiality of mutual enrichment.

As a member of the Independent group, and as a practising clinician, my work is informed by my patients' experience of their minds and bodies in both their inner and outer worlds, and I try to understand the interaction between my patients and myself in terms of the celebrated dictum of Joan Riviere, the analyst of Donald Winnicott, who would say to students in supervision when they presented her with some brilliant intellectual construction "Very well, but who is doing what to whom with what organ?"

One may also pose the question in an inverse direction. "What has philosophy to teach the clinician?" I quote René Major's magisterial account of Derrida's philosophical position here (Major, 2000). Major says that for Derrida—perhaps the most eminent and sympathetic philosophical discussant of psychoanalysis in France at the moment—

> Psychoanalysis—its theory, its practice, its institution, is wholly a science of the archive and of the proper name, of a logic of hypomnemesis which explains the lacunae of memory, of what archives memory by transforming it, or anarchivizes, erases or destroys it: it is also the science of its own history, of that of its founder, of the relation between private or secret documents and the elaboration of its theory and of everything which in a subterranean manner can enlighten its appearance in the world. [*ibid.*, p. 3]

In my terms. I think that Derrida is speaking about splitting and repression as central to mental process, but I would need more time to expand on this thesis.

In Derrida's definition there is no mention of the body (Freud said that the Ego is first and foremost a body Ego), so that the teaching of Joan Riviere would seem to have little place in the Derridarean theory of psychoanalysis. As a practising analyst, which Derrida is not, this placed me in a dilemma. How would I put such a philosophically based theory into practice? Indeed, how much should abstract theorizing enter into the way in which I formulate my interpretations and understand the transference?

To illustrate the point I wish to make, let me turn to a patient who has been in five times a week analysis with me for the last seven years. My work with her has been greatly enriched by my reading of Shakespeare's last complete play, *The Tempest*. This patient, Hannah, was twenty-one years old when referred to me for analysis after various behavioural attempts to treat her severe anorexia had broken down. When she first came to see me she was very thin and pale, monosyllabic, and refused to look at me. She spoke only in a very low and monotonous tone and in appearance was completely androgynous.

Hannah's mother had had a previous marriage and had had a son and daughter by this marriage. She had divorced her first husband and subsequently had lived a very free life with numerous lovers, including Hannah's father. I doubt if she wished to marry again, but she fell pregnant and married Hannah's father some six months before Hannah was born.

Hannah had been born after her Mother had been rushed to hospital needing an emergency Caesarian section: the cord was round Hannah's neck and she had to be resuscitated at birth. Having been unconscious during the birth, her mother clearly had great difficulty in visualizing her and in treating her as a live baby, and indeed has never found a proper distance from her in their relationship. Instead, much of Hannah's infancy was taken over by her fifty-year-old father, whose first child she was. He is a very sadistic and controlling man, and he treated the new baby as an extension of himself and the recipient of numerous part object projections. As an example of his need to control, early in the analysis he tried to insist that I informed him of everything that was happening in the analysis, and when I refused to disclose the contents of our sessions, reported me to the President as behaving improperly. He was furiously angry when he was told that this was indeed appropriate in an analysis and subsequently did all he could to sabotage Hannah's treatment. Winnicott remarks that

> There is in cases of failure of environmental responsibility, an alternative danger, which is that this potential space may become filled with what is injected into it from someone other than the baby. It seems that whatever is in this space that comes from someone else is persecutory material, and the baby has no means of rejecting it. [1971, p. 120]

As the contemporary British poet Philip Larkin puts it (Larkin, 1988)

> They fuck you up, your mum and dad.
> They may not mean to but they do,
> They fill you with the faults they had
> And add some extra just for you.

Hannah's mother reports her as having been a very lusty baby who was always ravenous. When she was three months old, her mother left her with carers and went on a prolonged holiday with her new husband as a way of compensating herself for what she had given up. Hannah was left in the care of a nanny who was kind to her and tried to meet her needs. She remained difficult to feed and would scream if she felt that she had not had enough to eat. Eventually, on his return, her father intervened and insisted that she be shut away in the kitchen at night so as not to disturb his sleep. Her response was to become addicted to the kummel (a liqueur) which she was given to quieten her when her teeth began to erupt and she carried a bottle with her as a pacifier until she was two. Her father then intervened again and insisted on throwing her bottle out of the window and denying her any more of her " stuff" as she called it.

There then began a long period of battle with her environment. She was very identified with her father, the aggressor, and refused to wear feminine clothes, always insisting on being dressed in shorts or trousers. She seems to have spent little time with her mother, who rather abandoned her to nannies, but a great deal of time with her father, who made a confidante of her and treated her as a special child, which she found very gratifying. A sister, Jessie, was born two years later, but she seems to have had a much more normal birth and upbringing and reports no traumata. Hannah always has felt very responsible for her sister, who is pretty and feminine, and cared for her and looked after her at all times. Although she likes her elder half-sister, and they get on well, she is much closer to Jessie, and for the last few years they have very companionably shared a flat in London.

When Hannah was six years old her father began systematically to abuse her sexually, including forcing her to fellate him: this continued in secret for some five years. She never disclosed the abuse to anyone, but grew up as a little strange creature who was neither boy nor girl. Hannah was highly intelligent and seemed very far-sighted, so that she would be consulted by her relations on all kinds of problems: she was regarded in the family as a "wise child". She refused to follow the usual middle-class precepts concerning success in games and competitiveness and kept herself very much to herself. She occasionally could rebel openly, as when she turned on a sprinkler while her mother was holding a lunch party for some ladies and soaked them all. She had but one friend, a mixed-race boy, which greatly shocked her parents, but she adamantly refused to give him up. She describes one occasion when she was swimming in the family swimming pool and allowed herself to sink to the bottom and just lay there looking at the surface. She was in no way distressed and felt that she wanted to remain there forever, but fortunately her father was nearby and dived in and brought her to the surface again before she lost consciousness. I think that this was a way of telling those close to her about her internal world, and that she was suffering from a psychotic illness that was not recognized by her environment.

Both parents were alcoholic and, with hindsight, it was clear to her that their sexual relationship was very bad. Hannah was intensely curious about what was happening in the parental bedroom and would often try and catch them unawares if they were making love. On one occasion she found menstrual blood on the sheets but her mother, instead of enlightening her, passed it off as nothing. She dates her intense guilt about her parents' sexual relationship and her feeling that she was the cause of the difficulty from this time, and linked it in her material with a memory of her father bellowing at her mother that he would fuck her or bugger her any time that he wanted to.

During the first eighteen months of analysis many memories of this type surfaced, but it was difficult to link these memories convincingly with her anorexia. Sent to boarding school at twelve, she became a juvenile rebel—and then when her menses began at fifteen she decided to refuse food. She did this secretly and successfully for nearly a year, and began to be imitated by other girls, so that when the school discovered the reason for her weight loss and the effect that it was having on her schoolmates, they insisted that her parents take her away. She had become so ill that she had to be hospitalized and in fact was close to death. Her mother took her to live at home where she could oversee her feeding, and she went to school locally. There was intense conflict with both parents over food, but generally she was able to impose her wishes on the situation. She was hospitalized more than once and had both physical and psychological treatment. With hindsight she can see that this was a refusal to accept a woman's body and sexuality. She felt intensely guilty about her parents and their relationship and blamed herself excessively for their difficulties. To try to cure her anorexia she was sent to various treatment regimes, became clinically depressed, was given many ECTs and antidepressants, and nearly died from self starvation on several occasions. Yet, on occasions, when in the hospital under a behaviourist regime, she felt very calm and serene: when she was kept in her room and allowed no privileges if she did not eat, she did not mind the isolation. In a way it absolved her from her guilt and her conflicts; it was lying at the bottom of the swimming pool. She also had a great disillusionment in that one of the nurses befriended her and she felt that she had someone who cared for her, but when the hospital became sceptical about her cure and gave her ECT the nurse who had promised to be her friend deserted her. Because the doctors no longer knew what to do with her, she was then sent to an old-fashioned asylum, so that eventually she found herself on a ward that was a dump for incurable psychotics. Her father was informed and immediately removed her—she remembers saying to him at the time, "I won't tell". Eventually, at the recommendation of a visiting eminent psychiatrist, she was sent to this country for an analysis that was not available where she lived. The psychiatrist gave her parents my name, I was asked if I would treat her, and I accepted her as a patient on the essential condition that she had proper medical supervision. My friend and colleague, Dr X very kindly consented to provide this for her. I can quite categorically say that without Dr X's constant support Hannah would undoubtedly have died. During the first months of the analysis she monitored Hannah's weight and was always available to her when she was living alone and when, as we will see, Hannah became both psychotic and suicidal, she could call Dr X, who was prepared to visit her at home at any time of day or night. She admitted Hannah to hospital when she overdosed, and convinced the emergency room of the need to resuscitate her. I am quite clear that the care her physician provided helped Hannah to change her view of herself into one of a valuable and worthwhile person. For myself, the analysis would have been frankly impossible if I had not been able to telephone Dr X at any time, not only for the valuable insights which she was able to give me, but to ask her to intervene in a way that my analytic role made imposssible for me when I believed Hannah's life and survival were at risk.

There are many ways in which Hannah's illness might be understood. But my interest in this paper is to demonstrate a hermeneutic link from the analysis to one of the last plays by Shakespeare—*The Tempest*. It is not my intention to offer a "psychodynamic" account of the play or to encroach on the ground of literary criticism. For those interested there are typical papers easily available in the literature, e.g., Sokol (1993), who offers a rather clumsy "Kleinian" account of the play, or Ellman (1994), who links Lacanian ideas and recent critical notions. While these are interesting and worthwhile areas of academic study, my intention in this paper is to show how two very different theories interacted in me to enable me better to understand the clinical problems with which I was dealing.

The play was recently revived in London at Shakespeare's Globe Theatre, with the distinguished actress Vanessa Redgrave playing the part of Prospero. I thought this experiment in cross-gender acting was not a success. When I saw the play it became forcibly apparent that Prospero needs to be played by a man, for reasons that will appear in my account of the play. I shall focus here on some of the attributes of Prospero's role in the play with which I identified when I stood with my son—a distinguished interpreter of the role of Caliban in England and the United States—among the groundlings in the pit in the recreation of the old Elizabethan theatre.

Some years ago I had published an account of the play in the *International Review of Psychoanalysis* (Hildebrand, 1988) and my later approach to the issues I consider in this paper is based on that work. To summarize, the action of *The Tempest* takes place on a desert island, where Prospero the magician and rightful Duke of Milan and his daughter Miranda have dwelt alone apart from Caliban, a savage, and Ariel, a spirit, since being exiled there by Prospero's usurping brother Antonio when Miranda was an infant. Using magic arts, Prospero conjures up a storm that wrecks his brother Antonio, Alonso the King of Naples, his son Ferdinand, and Alonso's brother Sebastian on the island. The action consists of the foiling of various plots conducted both by Antonio and Sebastian and by Caliban and the king's drunken butler and jester against the lives of the rightful rulers Alonso and Prospero: meanwhile, Miranda and Ferdinand fall in love. With the aid of his familiar spirit, Ariel, Prospero achieves a solution that enables him to regain his Dukedom, to marry his daughter to the King's son, to foil the various plots, and redress the wrongs he has suffered at the hands of the usurper Antonio. The play is in the form of a Romance and, like *Hamlet*, contains a play within a play. As I pointed out in my paper "Shakespeare here reworks the previous themes of *Hamlet* in a different sense—the murder of the king while sleeping is foiled by magic means, the warring brothers are—ostensibly—reconciled— and the lovers united" (Hildebrand, 1988, p. 35). Summarizing Hamlet in this way does not do justice to the intricacy of the verse or the subtlety of the drama.

When thinking about Hannah's analysis in the context of my reading of *The Tempest*, I could identify her partly with the virgin Miranda, who has never seen a man apart from her father and the sexually voracious monster Caliban, and partly as the asexual Ariel. Like Susannah in *The Marriage of Figaro*, Miranda's emergence into sexual maturity provides one of the mainsprings of the action. As I argued in my previous paper on *The Tempest*, Prospero, while being the protagonist of the action of the play, and whose magical gifts compel the other characters to do as he commands, is himself under no illusion: if the exile on the island has been his withdrawal into philosophical study and magical omnipotence, while protecting this his daughter, through their isolation, from sexuality and hostility, he must at the conclusion of the play return to the real world and release his daughter from the Oedipal bond; this denouement will lead to his end—"my every third thought shall be of death". Moreover, he can also finally release Ariel—the Imaginary is transformed at last into the Symbolic—reluctantly but for good. Prospero will return to Milan and to the humdrum daily round. That this may be a disaster is, of course a danger that he cannot ignore, but if he wants to hand on both the succession and allow sexual potency to his daughter and her husband, this, in reality, is the only choice that he can make. Acceptance of one's own mortality is the only possible life-giving choice that will secure the dynasty. Nothing could be harder-headed than Prospero's decision—nothing further from the holocaust at the end of *Hamlet*. Where René Major, in his studies of the proper name, speaks of the "de-nomination of Hamlet", perhaps in *The Tempest* we should speak of the "nomination" of the children who are to succeed and make their way in the world at whatever cost to the elders.

To return to Hannah, after eighteen months of analysis Hannah disclosed her experiences of abuse by her father to me—the memory of which she had never completely repressed—and an extremely painful period of her life began. She had given me many hints before in the form of memories of having been abused by waiters while on holiday and assaulted by twin brothers at a family wedding when she was a child. She produced these memories with great difficulty and enormous pain. I did not know at that time how to understand and interpret these memories: this was at a time when the controversies about recovered memory were at their height and, although of course acknowledging how painful this was for her, I found it hard to see quite how best to interpret this very delicate and difficult material. I now regard the memories as examples of *nachtraglichkeit* (deferred action) and suspect that they were indirect ways of making me aware of the problems of sexual abuse in her inner world without directly implicating her actual father. After many halting attempts, she told me of the abuse that her father had offered her and we began to work on the material. As I say, I had no way of knowing at this time whether this was truth or fantasy, but I did feel that the circumstantial nature of the memories that she was offering me was far more convincing, particularly in terms of what I knew of him, than the earlier scenarios. Later, another father figure—a Mr McGregor, who was a foreman on a local farm whom she claimed had witnessed a scene of sexual abuse between her father and herself and had then forced her to fellate him—was added to the story, but again I suspect that these were displaced ways of dealing with her intense anger and guilt about what had happened and the need to reveal it in the transference. Indeed, the relationship through the name to the Peter Rabbit stories made me suspect that this was her way of telling me the pain that she was experiencing in the transference in informing me about the abuse. I naturally took this up with her, that I, too, had become the abusing father watching what was going on and using my knowledge to manipulate her and abuse her in the transference, but to little or no apparent effect since she insisted on the veracity of her memory and insisted on splitting off the transference implications.

After some time, Hannah took advantage of a parental visit to this country to inform her mother, who had always shut her eyes to any awareness of the abuse, and the whole family reluctantly became involved in the problem. She also told Dr X, who suggested a family conference with a psychologist who set up a family confrontation in the course of which her father denied everything and strode out of the room threatening that he would sue everyone involved. Following this encounter, which shook her enormously, Hannah entered a period of frank psychosis: she hallucinated voices and cruel mocking faces, hid from me in various corners of the consulting room, was terrified of what was emerging from her inner world: she would on occasions faint on leaving my house and she was often exceedingly paranoid, and she felt that she had to control all her thoughts and actions to protect herself from the attacks of others. The only people she claimed she trusted were her doctor and myself. She had always been a self mutilator, although her family had always scotomized the cuts on her arms, and she now cut her wrists almost daily. While I kept as strictly as possible to the analytic regime, I felt that it was necessary for me to be available to her by telephone at any time of day or night.

She also had times when she would become so guilty and responsible for the abuse that she felt she should die. It became her practice to telephone me in the country at weekends and tell me that she had taken an overdose so that I could let her doctor or the police know and they could get her into hospital where we could tell them that she had informed us of her intentions and therefore the emergency room would resuscitate her rather than letting her die, as is now becoming the practice in some hospitals in England. Winnicott (1971), speaking of a patient similar to Hannah, says

> She feels when people are hopeful about her that they are expecting something of her and this brings he up against her essential inadequacy—all this is a matter of intense grief and resentment to the patient and there is plenty of evidence that without help she would be in danger of suicide, which would simply have been the nearest thing that she could get to murder. If she gets near to murder she begins to protect her object so that at that point she has the impulse to kill herself and in this way to end her difficulties by bringing about her own death and the cessation of the struggle. Suicide brings no solution, only cessation of the struggle. [p. 33]

Dr X and I, as caring parents, had to be hopeful about her and she had to try and destroy our hope in her and the outcome of our work together.

I would visit her in hospital when she was an inpatient and continued the analysis there as strictly as was possible until she was discharged. She dreamt frequently, except when on psychotropic drugs, and much of the work was based on her dream material. A typical dream at this time was

> she was at the circus. She was very small. There were lions in the big cage. Strings of vines were growing through her nose and her ears and she kept breaking them off. A ringmaster came round and took her on to the stage, but the vines kept growing and everyone cheered. At the entrance to the tent her father was standing He was naked and she just looked at him. She asked him to break off all these stems but he just stood there and did nothing.

Her associations were about a visit to the circus with her father when she was a child. She had been given a comic mask and later he had forced her to fellate him while he was wearing the mask, which he had taken from her. I thought that the vines were the projections that were being forced into her and her feeling of public exposure now that the reality of the abuse was known to the world. The lions were her caged anger with the men—her father and myself—who put her in this position and did nothing to try and understand her shame and pain at being used in this way. She felt as powerless now to disappear from sight or sink to the bottom of the pool as she had been when she was small. No one could be trusted to know and understand her true feelings and her needs. She was saying, in Winnicott's terms, that there was no room in her for the development of a potential space, a space that could not exist because "there was never a built up sense of trust matched with reliability and therefore no relaxed self realization" (*ibid*. p.171).

Nevertheless, we battled on, and there were longish intervals when she was not overtly psychotic, going round in a fairly continuous cycle of despair and self questioning on her part and a need to test my interpretations and what she felt to be my unjustified hope about her almost to (self) destruction. However, she did gradually reduce the number of hospitalizations and she and Jessie, who had come to London to study, lived fairly contentedly together. She had also acquired a cat—plainly a transitional object with whom she could feel love and closeness in a way that she felt was impossible with human beings. She is a very determined person and, having undertaken a higher degree, she managed, despite her difficulties, to achieve a distinction, which brought great pleasure to her family and to her therapeutic team, if not to Hannah herself.

Progress was slow and halting, but eventually, some nine months ago, she decided that enough was enough, stopped taking the antipsychotic and antidepressant drugs prescribed by her psychiatrist, now eats moderately but adequately, and has stopped mutilating herself. She is still distressed if she cannot remember the beginning of a train of thought, or forgets something that she has seen. I do not know why the psychotic episodes ceased as they did: I cannot point to any one interpretation or series of interpretations that might account for this. I should add that she remained seriously ill; but she never willingly missed a session and the work continued at all times.

Hannah has always called me Dr H—I have no proper name in her inner world. I suppose that I might be called "a transitional analyst". I believe that I became in the transference a non-abusing father, a sort of magical Prospero who allowed her to communicate and contemplate her feelings and her despair within a reliable and protected environment. When she was a baby she always cried a lot because she was so hungry, so her father decided that he was not to be dictated to by this child and would leave her in her cot in the kitchen to cry all night where he need not be woken by her. In contrast, I became in her inner world a feeding breast that she could both use and attack through her acting in and out without retaliation or the need for excessive splitting and projection, as when I gave her permission to call me in the night when she was suicidal and took effective action to respond to her mental state.

Her father had been badly abused himself as a child, and plainly used her as a surrogate for the hurt and abused little boy inside himself. Although he put enormous pressure on her to come to see him, and also threatened to visit her in London, she was gradually able to disregard his demands. By now refusing to meet him she felt that she was able to discard his projections and reclaim her own individuality, and the possession of her own mind and body. I was also a mother with whom she could communicate, although with great pain, about the penetrating attacks on her body and her mind, and who would feed her with ideas and interpretations that were not necessarily persecuting, although she could not identify with me as a sexual being of either gender. Close physical contact with anything other than her pet cat, Jake, was impossible for her. Since we do not shake hands with our patients in England, I have had no physical contact with her throughout her analysis, and when she would faint on my staircase or be unable to leave the consulting room, fortunately I was always able to call on the assistance of my wife to (literally) handle her and meet her needs. This is the Ariel aspect of her character.

To return to the play, it is, of course, essential to underline that the characters of *The Tempest* are not real people, but represent a powerful web of internal relationships that the dramatist has staged on our behalf. Frank Kermode, in his recent elegant essay on the language of Shakespeare, notes that when it comes to Caliban, the savage man, there are clear echoes of the parent–child conflict (Kermode, 2000).

PROSPERO: I indowed thy purposes
        With words that made them known. But thy vild race

(though thou didst learn) Had that in it which good
natures
Could not bear to be with.

to which, Caliban replies "Thou taught me language, and my profit
on't is, / I know how to curse."

(Given Lacan's statement that the unconscious is structured like
a language, I wonder what a Lacanian analyst would have made of
that interchange?)

It is a tenable hypothesis that in reading Shakespeare we can
discover through his language the dramatic expression of the vicissitudes of anger, desire, and envy directed at our objects in our
inner worlds and the need to split off and defend against them. Not
only is *The Tempest* concerned with the projection of rage and sexuality into the younger man, as expressed in the split in Prospero's
attitude between the acceptable Ferdinand and the monster
Caliban, but also the problem of the older man and the adolescent
girl and his sexual power over her and his reluctance to give up this
potency and accept the end of his reign, while she turns to other,
younger men and to potential motherhood. Again, the fraternal
conflict ends disastrously in *Hamlet*, and Lear erupts into madness
as he tries to continue to maintain his *jouissance* over his daughters.
The *Tempest*, being a Romance, resolves these issues rather less trag-
ically—nevertheless, Prospero dismisses Antonio with the deepest
contempt (*vide* Auden's wonderful gloss on the play in *The Sea and
the Mirror* (Auden, 1944)), but one cannot doubt that these issues
and their resolution are being continuously being worked through
by the poet.

Frank Kermode recalls that Henry James described *The Tempest*
as a "disciplined passion of curiosity". Kermode feels that the
linguistic discipline of the play is extraordinary.

> The irruptions of Ariel, for whom, as for Caliban a *new* dramatic
> language had to be invented, the pervasiveness of music, the quiet
> verbal insistence on dream, on spirit, on sea give *The Tempest* qual-
> ities which are in the end beyond description. [Kermode, 2000, p.
> 300]

For the analyst the hermeneutic, the interpretation of the play,
must lie with the way in which it expresses and underlines implied

object relationships and their integration into new mental structures, particularly those to do with the acceptance and recognition of aggression, reparation, and the reintegration of split off parts of the self, as expressed so beautifully by Kermode, together with the renunciation of *jouissance* and omnipotent sexual control by Prospero at the conclusion of the action.

Indeed, even Caliban can react to the beauty of the island, as when he says to the clowns,

CALIBAN: Be not afeard, the isle is full of noises,
            Sounds, and sweet airs, that give delight and hurt not.
            Sometimes a thousand twangling instruments
            Will hum about mine ears, and sometimes voices,
            That if I then had wak'd after long sleep,
            Will make me sleep again, and then in dreaming,
            The clouds methought would open, and show riches,
            Ready to drop upon me, that when I waked
            I cried to dream again. (3.2: 138–146)

And of course he, too, learns that there is more to life and language than cursing. His last words in the play are "I will be wise hereafter and seek for Grace".

Let me turn now back to Hannah. Here one aspect of her struggle to free herself from her very destructive internal objects lies in the action of the analytic work. It seems plausible to suggest that she was able to give up her illness through the internalization of the analytic relationship and the replacement of intensely sadistic and cruel internalized object relations and her defences against them by much more reparative and less compulsive behaviours. Is all well then? This cannot yet be said. Despite the excellent results so far, more work needed to be done.

Having reached this moment of change and growth, there were changes in my own health just before Christmas of 2000, which led me to tell the majority of my patients that it was my intention to retire. I had held back with Hannah because of her evident fragility following her decision to give up her illness, and a fear that she might relapse into psychosis. There was clear evidence in her analytic material that she was unconsciously aware that I was ill (she gave me a book called *Darwin's Worms*, which is intensely centred on death and reparation, as a Christmas present). Eventually my health became so fragile that I decided that I could no longer avoid the decision. I had long felt that if I retired, then she should go to a woman analyst, and I knew that an old friend and colleague who was well acquainted with my manner of working would be happy to take her on.

It was very painful to tell Hannah of my decision and the reason behind it, which was that I could not promise her to remain alive for the time that would be required to help her through the next stage of our work, which I thought meant her coming to terms with her own sexuality and her own gender. I had a lot of material to support this in the form of dreams and associations about her body, about her having a child—something she had never been able even to contemplate before—and the emergence of memories and the reworking of her feelings at school when she had begun to menstruate.

She was aghast at first, and said that she didn't think that she could go to anyone else since no one had ever listened to her as I had done. She had a brief period of depression and mutism in the analysis. I made it clear that there was no way I was going to force her to go elsewhere and the choice was entirely hers: but I could not go back on my decision to stop the analysis. Her reply was very illuminating—she said that the problem did not lie there, but in her realization that her suicidal attempts must have been enormously painful for those close to her and for me. For the first time she could emerge from her solipsistic world and realize the pain that her suicidal behaviour must have caused to those who cared about her. She also felt that her struggles with her inner world must be far less than mine, compared to those of me and my family in facing the imminent prospect of my own death, and that she felt she could now get her difficulties into a better perspective.

A few days later she brought me a vivid dream: a seed had been forced into her mouth against her will and it had turned into a sunflower inside her. Tendrils of the plant had grown out of her mouth and nose and ears and she had felt enormously attacked and had awoken with feelings of terror. Her associations to this dream—which of course was a reworking of the dream I reported earlier in the chapter, were very interesting: she recounted for the first time in this long analysis that when she was nearly two she had had an operation on her mouth because there was a gum flap joining the inside of her lips to the gum above her front teeth. She had resisted the general anaesthetic, screaming, and the nurses had not been able to hold her. Her father had held her down while the assault was made on her mouth.

I interpreted the link between the attacks on her mouth, the fellatio, and her feeling that I was now both cutting off the good analytic feed and forcing her to have a sexual intercourse and an oral child that she did not wish to accept. This interpretation made it possible for her to look more calmly at her situation and to express more clearly both her anger and her guilt about my illness, which would mean the end of our analytic relationship. She has been able to telephone her future analyst and arrange to meet her while we work towards a termination at the end of the summer.

Part of my thinking about Hannah has had to do with projective identification. As I have had to delay the publication of this account for reasons of health, I shall add one small anecdote to this history. I think that it partakes somewhat of magic and the uncanny. As I have said, Hannah's cat Jake was very much the repository of her good objects. In thinking about Hannah and Jake I was often reminded of a paper by my own analyst, Beryl Sandford, entitled "A patient and her cats", in which she recounts the very concrete way a psychotic patient would bring her cats to the consulting room to express split off and destructive parts of the patient and how she would go to tea with this patient when once again the cats would be used as the repository of unwanted feelings about the analyst, both positive and negative (Sandford, 1966). Imagine my feelings, then, when a week after Hannah was due to start analysis with her new analyst, she called me to say that Jake had been run over and killed on the actual day of the first session and that she had therefore postponed starting for a week. Her question to me was—should she buy another cat, since the pain of loss was so great! Despite being greatly tempted to interpret, I confined myself to saying that I thought she should get a new cat once she had worked through her mourning.

For me, the link between Hannah and *The Tempest*, the link that has enriched our work together, lies in Prospero's painful acceptance of his own anger and pain at the loss of his omnipotent power as the Master of the island and his capacity to contemplate the imminence of his own death. This feeling was particularly clear when I was a spectator at the play, as I have described, and I could experience my own identification with Prospero when he says

PROSPERO: {.} graves at my command
              Have waked their sleepers, oped, and let 'em forth
              By my so potent art. But this rough magic
              I here abjure, and when I have required
              Some heavenly music—. . . . which even now I do . . .
              To work mine end upon their senses
              That this airy charm is for, I'll break my staff,
              Bury it certain faddoms in the earth,
              And deeper did ever plummet sound
              I'll drown my book. (5.1: 48–57)

It is very hard for the analyst to give up his powers, something that came home to me when I did a literature search and found how little had been written concerned with the impact of the disappearance or death of the analyst on his patients, and how few patients had had the possibility of some working through beforehand. The Lacanian notion that the patient treats the analyst as "Le sujet supposé savoir"—the person who will know and be able to cure what is wrong with him or her—an assumption that all patients have to painfully surrender in order to effect a cure and take control over their own lives and their inner worlds as much as is possible seems very apposite here. I feel that I had perhaps for too long been such a person in the analysis for Hannah, and that her painful disillusionment that I was no more omniscient or immortal than any one else may have been, in view of all that had happened between us, very therapeutic. Analysts, as I have discovered, have to return to Milan and the real world and the withdrawal into study and magic has to be abandoned if one is to be real for oneself as well as for one's patients. I have no idea what will happen to Hannah in the future—that is no longer in my hands—but in surrendering my analytic role, I hope that she may be able be in touch with the possibility of using her potential as fully as she may wish.

Finally, to return to my theme. I have suggested in this brief clinical anecdote that literature and psychoanalysis can enrich one another as complementary hermeneutics and that it is possible for an analytic experience, providing it does not try to go beyond the single case method, to promote this process. I feel that philosophical systems, fascinating as they are in their theoretical elaborations, are secondary for the clinician, who is dealing with the interplay of phantasy and reality in the inner world. I wish that there had been more time to elaborate on this difficulty. That they can explain *ex post facto* I have no doubt. For the present I have still to be convinced that they have much use to me in the heat of the analytic process, and that I do not and cannot think in such terms as I work with patients.

Notes

1. The title of this paper may seem somewhat mystifying. To explain, some time ago I was invited to contribute a short paper to the proceedings of the Estates Generaux of Psychoanalysis, which were to be held in Paris in July 2000. The aim of the meeting was to provide a forum for psychoanalysts of all schools in which they could discuss their theoretical and scientific theory and practice free from the stultifying rivalries and bureaucracies that have laid a dead hand on so many congresses organized by the IPA.

    What particularly gratified me in this invitation was that it gave me the opportunity to speak at the Sorbonne, my own University, and from the platform in the Grand Amphitheatre where, as a student in the years 1948–1951, I had had the pleasure and privilege of attending lectures by such great psychologists as Maurice Merleau-Ponty and Jean Piaget.

References

Auden, W. H. (1944). *The Sea and the Mirror, A Commentary on Shakespeare's* The Tempest. A. Kirsch (Ed.). Princeton, NJ: Oxford University Press, reprinted 2003.

Benvenuto, S. (2000). Relations of psychoanalysis with the sciences. In: *Contributions to Estates General of Psychoanalysis, Journal of European Psychoanalysis, 10–11;* www.psychomedia.it/jep

Ellmann, M. (Ed.) (1994). *Psychoanalytic Literary Criticism.* New York: Longman.

Felman, S. (1977). Turning the screw of interpretation. In: S. Felman (Ed.), *Literature and Psychoanalysis: The Question of Reading.* Baltimore: Johns Hopkins University Press.

Hildebrand, P. (1988). The other side of the wall. *International Review of Psycho-analysis, 15*: 353–362.

Kermode, F. (2000). *Shakespeare's Language.* London: Penguin.

Kott, J. (1967). *Shakespeare Our Contemporary.* London: Methuen.

Larkin, P. (1988). *Collected Poems.* London: Faber.

Major, R. (2000). Desintentiel psychoanalysis. In: *Contributions to the Estates General of Psychoanalysis, Journal of European Psychoanalysis, 10–11*; www.psychomedia.it/jep

Sandford, B. (1966). A patient and her cats. *Psychoanalytic Forum, 1*(2):

Shakespeare, W. (1623). *The Tempest.* London: Arden.

Sokol, B. J. (1993). *The Undiscovered Country: New Essays on Psycho-analysis and Shakespeare.* (Contains an annotated bibliography of recent books and articles on the topic.) London: Free Association Books.

Winnicott, D. W. (1971). *Playing and Reality.* London: Faber.

INDEX